D0685905

TALES OF TALIESIN
A MEMOIR OF FELLOWSHIP

Cornelia Brierly

Herberger Center for Design Excellence
in collaboration with
The Frank Lloyd Wright Foundation

Pomegranate
SAN FRANCISCO

Published by
Pomegranate Communications, Inc.
Box 6099, Rohnert Park, CA 94927

Pomegranate Europe Ltd.
Fullbridge House, Fullbridge
Maldon, Essex CM9 4LE, England

Catalog number A539
ISBN 0-7649-1335-2

© 2000 Arizona Board of Regents and The Frank Lloyd Wright
Foundation, Taliesin, Spring Green, Wisconsin, and Taliesin West,
Scottsdale, Arizona.

Julie A. Russ, Editor
Brenton Elmore, Cover design and book concept
Marilyn Benedict, Graphic consultant

Second edition. Originally published in 1999 by the Herberger Center
for Design Excellence, College of Architecture and Environmental
Design, Arizona State University, Tempe.

*All rights reserved. No part of this publication may be reproduced or transmitted in
any form or by any means, electronic or mechanical, including photocopy, recording,
or any information storage or retrieval system, without permission in writing from
the publisher, except in the case of brief quotations employed in review and similar
critical works. Every care has been taken to clear permission for the use of copy-
righted illustrations. In case of accidental infringement, copyright holders are asked
to write to the publisher*

PRINTED IN KOREA

08 07 06 05 04 03 02 01 00   10 9 8 7 6 5 4 3 2

To
Mr. and Mrs. Wright
and
the members of the Taliesin Fellowship
of
The Frank Lloyd Wright Foundation

CONTENTS

FOREWORD

In the late summer of 1932, twenty-three eager apprentices answered Mr. and Mrs. Wright's invitation to join them at Taliesin in Spring Green, Wisconsin. The Wrights' enticing and clarion call promised hard work, purpose, meaning, and achievement as the stultifying grip of the Great Depression tightened its chokehold on the future of talented and ambitious youths. Together, the Wrights and the apprentices embarked on a remarkable and successful journey: one that has achieved many mileposts and one that continues for succeeding generations.

Cornelia Brierly joined this dedicated band a scant two years after its beginning. She has remained at Taliesin for over three score years with only a brief time away to practice architecture with her husband. In most aspects she never went away and like the Wrights and the other giants—all major figures in *Tales of Taliesin* who formed the Taliesin Fellowship—she will never leave.

When the apprentices came to Taliesin in the early 1930s, most architects and critics shared the perception of Mr. Wright as a retiree who had already made his contribution through the Prairie School and other monuments like the Larkin Building, Unity Temple, and the Imperial Hotel. In a few short, but enormously active, years, he had harnessed a second major burst of creative energy punctuated by such great achievements as the Johnson Wax headquarters, Fallingwater, Taliesin West, Broadacre City, and the first Usonian houses. Apprentices learned their profession working on these buildings before leaving Taliesin to practice elsewhere. A few others, with the Wrights' encouragement, stayed at Taliesin. This group, including Cornelia Brierly, became the backbone of and continue the work of the Taliesin Fellowship.

No one, scholars and others alike, has definitively delineated the role of the apprentices and the Fellowship in stimulating and helping sustain Mr. Wright's utterly stupendous output in the last quarter century of his long life. But few, if any, doubt the existence of an important connection.

Cornelia Brierly's charming and lively *Tales of Taliesin* provides an intimate glimpse of life at Taliesin and of the men and women—and guests, children, and dogs, too—who made it a very special community. Her stories radiate their own warmth. They also provide insight into the larger questions about the role of the Fellowship in Mr. Wright's work.

The Taliesin Fellowship has changed (a process Mr. Wright called "The Eternal Law of Change"), as do all healthy, living organisms, in the years since his death in 1959 and the next twenty-five years when Mrs. Wright alone presided. Yet much remains of a leader's imprint, and Cornelia Brierly has herself become a major factor in the continuity. She helps keep many of the traditions alive and vigorous. Her *Tales of Taliesin*, itself, also provides a congenial record that will continue to inform the future.

Dr. H. Nicholas Muller III
President and CEO
The Frank Lloyd Wright Foundation

ACKNOWLEDGEMENTS

This book owes much to the collaborative efforts of many friends. Many of these stories, written over a period of time, appeared in our in-house weekly publication, *The Whirling Arrow*, edited and published by Dr. Joseph Rorke. Much of the early typing and computer work can be credited to June Hill, Liz Conn, and Sarah Robinson.

Dixie Legler, John deKoven Hill, and our CEO Dr. H. Nicholas Muller III read and made valuable contributions to the manuscript. Dr. Muller has spurred the process of publication and continued to help in every way.

Mrs. Myron Marty (Shirley) did a major job of the initial editing, sorting out, and organizing the material. Minerva Montooth helped in computerizing material. My daughter Indira Berndtson has been indefatigable in helping with all aspects of evaluating text, collecting photos, and managing other necessary tasks. Oscar Munoz has tirelessly searched for photos in the Archives of The Frank Lloyd Wright Foundation. Many Fellowship colleagues have also contributed photographs. Margo Stipe and Dan Watson contributed valuable computer expertise.

Jenkin Lloyd Jones, Charles Montooth, Ezra Stoller, Bruce Allison, Liz Conn, R. E. Deems, and Svetlana Alliluyeva Peters have graciously allowed the use of their letters.

For funding I am especially indebted to Arthur Bartley and Dr. Annette Beyer-Mears who started the ball rolling for publication. Others include Mr. and Mrs. Donald A. Schaberg, Mr. and Mrs. Quentin Blair, Mr. and Mrs. Loch Crane, Mr. and Mrs. Donald Stromquist, John Christian, and especially Mrs. Howard Barnett who capped the climax by ensuring coverage of publication costs.

I am especially grateful to Mr. and Mrs. Wright and all the members of our Fellowship who have shared in a remarkable life and without whom none of this would have taken place, and without whom I would have none of their stories.

I also wish to acknowledge Brenton Elmore for his concept design and my editor Julie A. Russ who has given tireless concern and thought to this book.

Finally, my sincere thanks to Arizona State University College of Architecture and Environmental Design and the Herberger Center for Design Excellence for having made this project come to light.

INTRODUCTION

Formal music concert at Taliesin, Wisconsin

Often when the cards are down, when the economic and educational systems of the country fail as they did in the Great Depression of 1929, some great idea or enterprise emerges as an awakening to a better way of life. Such a new approach took shape through the vision and inspiration of Mr. and Mrs. Frank Lloyd Wright in founding the Taliesin Fellowship in 1932. It became a fellowship of young aspiring architects from all parts of the world, anxious to become part of a fresh educational experience of learning by working together in an environment of creativity and beauty. These apprentices joined the Taliesin family, sharing the benefits of working and living side by side with two great leaders.

Frank Lloyd Wright and his wife Olgivanna Lloyd Wright found in beauty the highest form of morality and believed that architecture embraces all life, and so they formed the Fellowship with the idea of making a memorable circumstance of everyday events. The Fellowship began at Taliesin, the Wright's famous home in the hills of Spring Green, Wisconsin, forty miles west of Madison. For the apprentices the experiences of learning by doing—whether drawing in the studio, working on the farm, planting the garden, constructing buildings, sharing maintenance chores, singing in the chorus, or playing in the ensemble—became part of an intensely active and rewarding life at Taliesin.

Over the years young people came and went in a kaleidoscope of change. Working with the apprentices, Mr. and Mrs. Wright developed the potential of hundreds of young architects. For those of us who stayed, the bonds of many years of family sharing became extremely powerful. Over a period of more than six decades remarkable adventures and experiences have given rise to Taliesin folklore.

From these reminiscences, from these flashes of memory, I present *Tales of Taliesin*. Scholars and others have written a great deal about Mr. Wright's architecture but not about his broad view of architecture as it encompasses all life and how this became reality at Taliesin.

I arrived at Taliesin in 1934, two years after the Fellowship formed. The dynamic impact of this educational adventure changed the course of my life and has remained a continuing resource throughout the years. *Tales of Taliesin* captures some of my memorable experiences of this life and its people.

TALES OF TALIESIN

THE EARLY YEARS

Arrival At Taliesin

Photo of author taken by Mrs. Wright, 1935

In the fall of 1934, I arrived unannounced at the Spring Green, Wisconsin, depot shortly before midnight. The conductor dropped my trunk and suitcases onto the station platform. As the lighted train sped west, I was left stranded in darkness. After a long day's journey from my home in Pittsburgh, I arrived in this unlit, tiny village where I had ventured against the advice of my friends and professors but with the reluctant support of my two worried maiden aunts with whom I lived. I had come to join the Taliesin Fellowship, Frank Lloyd Wright's recently formed group for apprentice architects. Leaving my bags, I walked up the street until a light appeared in a second story window. Climbing a rickety wooden stairs, I landed in the telephone office. The operator, a large, substantial looking woman named Esther, looked me over. I said, "I'd like to call Taliesin."

"There's no one there," she replied. "They're all at Mrs. Porter's having a party." As I later learned, Esther, by listening in on all the party lines, knew the whereabouts of everyone. Also, her view from the second story window provided a vantage point from which to observe who came and went in the town. I pleaded with her, "Please try to call Taliesin; there may be someone there." Finally receiving an answer, she assured me I'd be picked up right away. Three people soon arrived at the station. They introduced themselves as Bruce Richards, Lucretia Nelson, and Blaine Drake (who later became my brother-in-law). They helped me into a hearse, a ponderous black conveyance named "Granny Botts," which they said they'd driven from the University of California in Berkeley.

This threesome triumphantly escorted me to Tan-y-deri, the house Mr. Wright had designed for his sister, Jane Porter, in 1907. My arrival completely surprised the assembled Fellowship. Later, I learned that all summer the group had speculated about me, the girl who had sent her tuition in the spring without a firm date of arrival. The music stopped; the square dancing stopped. A great fire crackled in the fireplace, casting a glow over the Japanese screen above the mantel and lighting the friendly faces around me. Antimony, bittersweet, and pine boughs hung from the mellowed wooden decks. The apprentices in their colorful fall clothes had been dancing an old-fashioned square dance called "Rufty Tufty."

Mr. Wright came to greet me. He wore a bright orange-red zinnia tucked into the pocket of his red suede vest, his tweed trousers buttoned at the ankles. Mrs. Wright wore a multicolored crocheted scarf over a blue jersey outfit with slacks that also buttoned at the ankles. When she came forward to speak to me, Mr. Wright said, "No, Mother, I'm talking to Cornelia." Mrs. Wright withdrew, but in that brief encounter she impressed me with her striking presence and the intense awareness of her dark eyes. In fact, the great presence of both Mr. and Mrs. Wright seemed to light the room. Great charm enhanced Mr. Wright's elegant, distinguished, and congenial manner.

Following my instincts

Mr. Wright asked where I'd gone to school. I told him I'd been studying architecture at Carnegie Tech but had left because of the uncreative classical Beaux Arts system taught there. I told him my professors first tried to discourage me from leaving, and then they wrote me off as a young radical embarking upon a complete misadventure. This apparently pleased Mr. Wright. He enjoyed the idea that I had rebelled against a stultifying situation.

Cornelia's room at Taliesin in Spring Green

During the spring of 1934, I had become disgusted with the architectural course at Carnegie Tech. At that critical time I had the good fortune to read Mr. Wright's refreshing, challenging *An Autobiography*, the story of a man who didn't copy the past, an architect who worked out new forms for a new age. He envisioned a different way of living and learning for the Taliesin Fellowship, an exciting holistic lifestyle for young aspiring architects.

Aside from reading Mr. Wright's autobiography, I knew nothing of him or of Mrs. Wright. My professors at Tech didn't seem to know about Mr. Wright or his work. The fact that by 1934 Frank Lloyd Wright had already altered the direction of architecture by his many masterpieces such as the Robie House, Unity Temple, Midway Gardens, Imperial Hotel, block houses in California, and others, seemed to have escaped them entirely. By following my own intuition or instinct I went to Taliesin and discovered the treasures of a life devoted to creative architecture, a life where beauty is held to be "the highest form of morality."

My sister, Hulda, who had just graduated from a course in painting and design, also applied to Taliesin—by sending her credentials—but didn't receive an answer. This discouraged her, but I determined to find a way to get there. By chance I met a friend who offered to send a letter of recommendation to Charlie Morgan, an associate of Mr. Wright. In a short time I received this letter:

"Come when the spirit moves."
Frank Lloyd Wright

Immediately I sent my $600 tuition, but being naive I waited until fall to go. For years afterwards I heard about apprentices like the Alden Dows, the William Deknatels, the Yen Liangs, and many others who had been there for the summer before I came and had just left. I had, unfortunately, missed the opportunity to know and work with them. But at last my life at Taliesin would become a reality. My unexpected arrival will always remain as a dream-like experience. It never occurred to me that I'd get off the train in the dark of a sleeping town; be driven in a hearse to the warm, colorful scene of the Fellowship enjoying an evening of music and dance at Tan-y-deri; and welcomed by Mr. and

Mr. and Mrs. Wright, 1952

Mrs. Wright, the two remarkable leaders with whom I had come to work.

After one long day's journey, my whole life changed. Little did I know that the friendly people I met that first night would become my lifelong family and that I would be part of Taliesin for the rest of my life. Soon after I had been established in the Fellowship, my sister Hulda came, too. Her first letter of application had never been received.

Mr. Wright personally supervised fixing up a room for me when I arrived—a golden room with a large stone fireplace, a band of windows overlooking the valley, and a door to a stone terrace. Little did I know that sixty years later I would still live in this valley and look out upon it with the same awe and sense of excitement that I did that day. This life has been richly rewarding, with unequaled friendships and experiences.

Getting to know Mrs. Wright

In the morning of my first day Mrs. Wright called me to her room. Her quiet but dynamic presence astonished me as she told about her childhood in Montenegro with her blind father, the Chief Justice. He liked to have her as his

Mr. and Mrs. Wright with grandson Brandoch Peters, 1952

companion, either to walk in the park or, at an early age, to read philosophical books to him. Mrs. Wright heard stories of her grandfather, a famous general and national hero whose armies saved Montenegro by defeating the Turkish aggressors. He trained Mrs. Wright's mother in military matters, and she became a general in the army, a military career that kept her away from home most of the time. When Mrs. Wright was nine years old, her father sewed a little pouch for his daughter's money and sent her to live with her sister, whose husband managed one of the czar's tea estates, to be educated in the Caucasus.

Later she studied at the czar's drama school in Moscow. When she returned to the Caucasus, she met Mr. Gurdjieff, a Near Eastern philosopher, and traveled with him to France where he established his Institute for the Harmonious Development of Man. While in Russia she married Vlademar Hinzenburg, an architect. They had one daughter named Svetlana. By the time Mrs. Wright came to United States in 1924, bringing Svetlana with her, she had already separated from her husband, as both their lives had taken different directions. Using her maiden name Olgivanna (Little John Anna) Lazovich, this vibrant young woman by chance met Mr. Wright

in a private box at the ballet in Chicago. As I listened, her story seemed like a fairy tale.

After our visit, she gave me the task of dusting the living room. I had never seen such a beautiful room, with broad windows overlooking a pastoral valley and the Wisconsin River beyond. I took my time enjoying the room as I dusted, although it was a golden autumn day and I would have preferred to be working with the apprentices who were harvesting winter vegetables from the garden and storing them in a mysterious root cellar.

Settling the valley

Mr. Wright's Lloyd Jones grandparents, who had emigrated from Wales, settled in the beautiful valley I saw from the living room windows. Their neighbors, the friendly Indians, liked to silently slip into their house at night to sleep by the fire, leaving venison or a sack of corn on the doorstep when they left in the morning. These Welsh grandparents were staunch Unitarians who brought with them the heritage of the Druids. The Druids, an ancient Celtic priesthood, revered trees and all nature, so Mr. Wright's uncles planted oaks and elms in their fields for the resting plowman and

decorated the family chapel with branches and flowers. The Lloyd Jones had ten children. Eventually the uncles bought farms in the valley. Mr. Wright's Aunt Jane and Aunt Nell started a progressive boarding school called Hillside Home School, and Mr. Wright's mother, Anna, married a very cultivated itinerant minister, William Cary Wright, who was also a musician.

From the beginning, Anna Wright determined her son Frank would become an architect and planned his young life accordingly. He developed an insatiable love of music from his father. The boy spent his summers on his uncles' farms where they kept him busy with chores and where he developed his muscles and a feeling for the land and nature. From this solid, well-rounded cultural background Frank Lloyd Wright developed the idealism and creativity to become a great architect who understood structures in a much larger context.

Fellowship life

The idea for the Taliesin Fellowship had come to Mr. and Mrs. Wright at the depth of the Depression in 1932 when Mr. Wright's architectural commissions had dribbled to zero. If there were no buildings to build, they thought, why not

Fellows at lunch. Taliesin, 1936
Left to right: Jack Howe, Hans Koch, Noverre Musson, Cornelia's sister Hulda, Blaine Drake, Burt Goodrich

build "builders of buildings"? Mr. Wright was then 65 years old, an age when most people retire. But he was as youthful and fit as a man half his age and full of creative energy.

After working out a plan for the new program, they sent out a circular inviting prospective apprentices to come and study architecture and the allied arts at their home, Taliesin, in Spring Green, Wisconsin. New apprentices would learn not only architecture but also construction, farming, gardening, and cooking, as well as the study of nature, music, art, and dance. They would learn to work with their hands, gaining knowledge of materials by building, sawing, and quarrying.

Maintenance chores would build character and a sense of responsibility.

Twenty-three young apprentices responded to the call, each bringing $600 to cover one year's tuition and room and board. Despite the fact that there was little money, under Mr. Wright's direction, the first apprentices repaired and added to existing buildings on the Taliesin property. From the abundant woods in the nearby hills, they cut timber for new construction, mined stone in the local quarries, burned limestone in the kiln to produce lime, and took sand from the river banks free for the digging.

Building on the past

When I arrived at Taliesin, the major building project then in progress was the drafting room, a large new addition to the Hillside Home School that Mr. Wright had built in 1902 for his aunts' progressive coeducational boarding school. After the school closed in 1916, the abandoned buildings deteriorated until Mr. Wright acquired them for the Fellowship. He designed a 5,000-square-foot drafting studio, converted the school's gymnasium into a theater, and added separate rooms for new apprentices at the sides of the drafting room.

Damn at Frank Lloyd Wright's Bungalow-Taliesin-near Spring Green, Wis.

Original postcard of the dam at Taliesin

Trusses of green oak timbers cut by the apprentices from the Taliesin woods had already been erected in the new drafting studio when I arrived. Mr. Wright called it an "abstract forest." An enormous stone fireplace, large enough to burn cord wood, dominated one end of the room. Part of the floor had been roughed in, but areas of flagstone remained. Apprentices learned to cut the stone in the quarry nearby and, under the instruction of a fine old Cornish stone mason, Charlie Curtis, they laid the new stone floor.

Learning by doing

All this construction was paralleled by intensive farm and garden work, a necessity in those days of financial hardship. Working alongside us, Mr. and Mrs. Wright taught us to garden, shuck corn, make hay, and thresh grain.

The dairy supplied whole milk for thirsty apprentices and cottage cheese, yogurt, and cream to be whipped or churned into butter. The chickens scratching in the sunny barnyard produced healthy eggs, and the animals browsing in the meadows furnished beef and pork that we smoked for ham and bacon. When the abundant vegetable garden had a surplus not needed for canning or for storing in the root cellar for winter, we marketed the produce.

Work proceeded with gusto and camaraderie and often with a spirit of competition, such as who could produce the largest pumpkin for the county fair. Everyone went to the fair, and we were sometimes rewarded with prizes for our produce. We earned prizes for a fat, milk-fed pumpkin, for a branch heavily laden with crab apples, our strawberry preserves, apple butter, cider, and for our superior animals.

The kitchen was the heart of Taliesin family life. In those early years, a large black iron stove dominated the ample space. The stove kept every cook busy stoking it with kindling wood, from four in the morning until the evening dinner. With no such things as thermostats or even oven thermometers, the cooks learned to hand-test the heat in order to turn out legions of loaves of bread, pies, cakes, roasts, and stews. In winter this friendly, beneficent stove made the kitchen a cozy gathering place, but in the hot, humid Wisconsin summers an apprentice could not find a steamier, more torrid work place.

Mrs. Wright taught all of us to cook with simplified dishes like stews of meat and vegetables or other inexpensive dishes that used our farm produce. However, from her translations of old Yugoslavian and Russian cookbooks of czarist days, we enjoyed a varied menu. For instance, a molded dish made of wheat berries, nuts, and cinnamon drops, called colieva, became a dish we served for afternoon teas. We also made golupsti, tiftilki, pirogi, blini, obertuk, Tsars' bread, and our traditional Easter dishes of Baba and pascha cheese. We cooked all these delicious recipes on the large wood-burning stove.

Many of us learned to cook by preparing cakes or cookies for tea. Once I tried to make doughnuts. They turned out so tough that Mr. Wright, with a twinkle in his eye, said, "Don't worry, Cornelia, everything that went into them was good!"

Starting the fire in the morning became the cook's responsibility, which often meant getting up at 4:00 A.M. on a freezing, black winter morning to stoke the stove. At the time, Taliesin had its own power provided by a hydroelectric plant installed by Mr. Wright on the dam at the base of the Taliesin hill. To turn on the lights, someone had to run down the hill through the snow to the dam and start the hydroelectric plant.

Besides the constant cooking and baking, canning the surplus produce started in early spring when luscious strawberries were made into preserves. As the season progressed, we made jelly and preserves from raspberries, blackberries, elderberries, and grapes. When properly made, one of our most delicious preserves was pavidla—made of damsen plums that we cut in half, sugared, and baked in the oven—a recipe from Mrs. Wright's childhood. Making pavidla was always a risky undertaking because, if overbaked, it ended up as a sticky unmanageable mass the consistency of roofing mastic, causing many in-family jokes about its possible uses.

Threshing oats, 1936
Left to right: Cornelia, Bitsy Gillham, Jack Howe, Maginel Wright Barney, Blaine Drake

Cornelia (right) and Bitsy Gillham threshing, 1936

As the summer season progressed we canned tomatoes, vegetable soup, green beans, corn, and varieties of pickles. We preserved the produce in two-quart jars; usually we canned two hundred jars of each. Once when I was cooking, two new apprentices, John Hill and Ben Masselink, infuriated me. They had tried to wash spinach in the washing machine and had chopped it to bits!

For many years the apartment just off the Hill Garden included a little dining room for Mr. and Mrs. Wright and a larger one for the Fellowship. The kitchen helper for the week served the Wrights. We regarded serving Mr. and Mrs. Wright and their guests as a pleasure and an honor. Each of us developed a special decoration for the dining room table. When Solomon Guggenheim, for whom Mr. Wright designed the Guggenheim Museum in New York, visited, I happened to be the server. My fall decoration included a brown linen tablecloth and an arrangement of old field balsam. Mr. Guggenheim expressed his appreciation and later while listening to music in the living room said, "This is the only place I've been where I have felt that culture is on every hand."

By fall, the root cellar, a large underground vaulted room with a sandy floor, overflowed with barrels of sauerkraut, shelves of canned tomatoes, corn, beans, fruit, and pickles. The bins around the walls contained fragrant apples, cabbage, Chinese cabbage, carrots, beets, rutabagas, onions, turnips, and varieties of squash, all of which lasted into the spring.

After the final frost, we browsed through the colorful autumn hills picking wild grapes or wild cherries for jam and wine. Stemming black cherries takes a lot of patience, but when they are thoroughly picked over, they can become a delicious liquor by packing them in a barrel, covering them with honey, sealing the keg with wax, and burying it in the sand of the root cellar until it ages. Manning the cider press and making apple butter provided two outdoor pleasures. We took turns sitting in the brisk fall air stirring apple butter as it burbled in the big black iron cauldron heated over a wood fire.

Bread and milk

One summer our garden produced a bumper crop of vegetables—carrots, beets, chard, spinach, peas, green beans, cabbage, tomatoes, squash, onions, potatoes, okra, lettuce, bell peppers, corn, and so on. We picked vegetables every morning. Each meal consisted of a variety of fresh, tender vegetables. To pick and prepare these required a lot of work. Mr. Wright, who always tried to find ways to minimize kitchen work in favor of outdoor or studio work, decided we would no longer prepare meals. Instead, the girls, dressed as milkmaids, would carry baskets of French bread and pitchers of milk to every workplace—whether to the workers fixing the dam, those shingling the roof, or others.

The "milkmaids" weren't happy with their role, as the baskets of bread and pitchers of milk were hard to manage. Working in the studio with bread in one hand and a paper cup of milk in the other, Mr. Wright expected workers to carry on their jobs without interruption. Trips to town each day to buy quantities of fresh bread became costly. Moreover, no matter how many chunks of bread and cups of milk were consumed people never felt satisfied and were apt to slip away to Spring Green for a better meal.

We no longer baked our good whole wheat bread, the garden vegetables died on the vine, and things like our homemade cottage cheese were no longer made. Mr. Wright ignored all our complaints about this experiment but continued for a week or so until he realized people were leaving their jobs to get a meal in town.

From the beginning Mrs. Wright had objected to the idea. She finally persuaded Mr. Wright in favor of our more healthy vegetables, whole wheat bread, and other farm products. I think by this time the whole idea had run its course, even with Mr. Wright, as it is probable that he also missed all the good farm food and quiet table service in their little dining room.

Tea time tradition

Throughout the summer and fall, afternoon tea was a great occasion. Taliesin has a historic Tea Circle: broad stone stairs rise from the courtyard garden to a semicircular stone seat under the protection of an ancient oak. Here Mr. and Mrs. Wright, apprentices, and guests gathered at four o'clock each afternoon to sip tea and enjoy one another's company. The conversation, often spiced by famous guests (Alexander Woollcott, Marc Connelly, Ludwig Mies Van der Rohe, and many others) stimulated discussions of architecture and philosophy. The Fellowship asked questions or contributed thoughts about Taliesin life. The tradition of the Tea Circle continued until just recently.

On the morning of June 18, 1998, a thundering storm violated our valley.

I've watched many Wisconsin storms, but never one of such magnitude. As I sat looking out of my courtyard room, the mighty Tea Circle Oak, which usually just flexed its foliage and limbs in a storm, succumbed to a wind of hurricane strength that drove leaves and branches in a straight line toward the Studio. Because of the roar of the storm, the uprooted tree seemed to fall noiselessly. The outreach of enormous limbs and foliage covered the courtyard and destroyed the Studio roof.

Mr. Wright's grandson, Brandoch, called our arborist, Bruce Allison, to dismantle our fallen giant. The whole Fellowship sat silently on the Hill Garden hill watching Bruce and his crew at their perilous job of dismembering this ancient spirit. Since 1933 it had sheltered generations of our Taliesin family.

Bruce Allison later wrote, "Using our biggest chain saw, I made the final cut into the prone lower trunk revealing the tree's recorded life history in stored annual rings. Two hundred twenty-five. The acorn had germinated in 1773 when the British ruled America: the oak was seventy-five years old when Wisconsin became a state in 1848: it was 94 when Frank Lloyd Wright was born in 1867: and it was 128 when Taliesin was built.

Scorch marks buried deep in the annual rings indicate that the oak had endured prairie fires, just as Mr. Wright had endured devastating fires at Taliesin in 1914 and 1924. Both tree and man had the strength to survive and continue to build."

Frances Nemtin has instigated an Arbor Day for Mr. Wright's birthday on June 8, 1999. With the help of the Fellowship, the Taliesin Preservation Commission, and the community, new trees will be planted throughout the Taliesin fields to usher in a new era and replace the many trees downed by storms.

Making the plan work

During the early years at Taliesin, Mrs. Wright carried the brunt of organizing activities—coordinating the work, planning meals, teaching people to cook, finding new recipes from her Russian and Serbian cookbooks, training people to work together, and managing the meager finances from Mr. Wright's occasional lecture tours, which accounted for most of the incoming cash. He received about $150 a lecture, a handsome honorarium in the 1930s, but not a great sum to sustain a growing family of young apprentices.

Tea time at the Tea Circle, 1937

Tea Circle without oak tree, October 1998

Ruth Blair pictured

Although the yearly tuition was very low, some apprentices could not meet it. During the Depression years, Mr. Wright was kind about accepting those who came without funds. To earn needed money, we often gave tours of Taliesin for interested visitors. Sometimes because of precarious finances we waited for a visitor's fifty-cent fee in order to buy much-needed flour. At that time during the Depression, however, one might find a hat or a dress in a bargain basement for one dollar.

It was a great responsibility for Mr. and Mrs. Wright to feed and house this large group of young apprentices now under their roof. But they also received great rewards in watching us grow, mature, and contribute to the effort of making this enterprise work. Our activities involved all sorts of unusual cooperative pleasures, such as cutting ice at the river in the winter to fill the ice house or making wine in the fall. By spring we filled the ice house, built with thick stone walls, with chunks of ice separated by layers of sawdust.

Mrs. Wright learned to make wine from the local farm ladies. This meant that sometimes we sat around the wine barrels in the sunny courtyard, squeezing grapes so that the purple juice streamed through our fingers while we laughed,
joked, and warded off bees that buzzed around the fragrant brew and wobbled drunkenly on the edge of the barrels.

Warming up the winters

Winters in Wisconsin have earned their reputation for severity. In order to keep the boilers going, the men worked in shifts day and night, stoking the boilers with four-foot logs. All the wood had to be sawed from the trees in the hills. Even we girls joined that detail. Our hired man, Ed Carmody, was so pleased to see me helping haul logs that he told our men, "She'd make some farmer a good wife!" What he didn't know is that I'd get so tired that occasionally I'd go off behind a bush and have a good cry to release my total exhaustion. But the snowy fields, little hummocks of brilliant bittersweet, or blue jays in the pines—and always, of course, the good humor, the jokes, and the laughter among friends—rewarded our efforts. In our leisure time we cross-country skied, ice skated, and tobogganed.

Indoors, Taliesin glowed with warm fires, as almost every room has a handsome stone fireplace. Some apprentices kept busy making architectural models. Others built new rooms, with Mr. Wright directing by waving his cane to point out
work to be done. Meanwhile, the girls got together and, with Mrs. Wright's instruction, made new bedspreads and curtains and knitted or crocheted afghans or scarves, or embroidered felt jackets with colorful yarn. Partners worked together to wind skeins of yarn, one swinging the yarn on outstretched arms while the other wound the ball. In such a relaxed setting, we developed a greater understanding of one another and friendships deepened. For Mrs. Wright it provided another way of studying the potential in each of us.

Then and now

During thunderstorms, I used to stand on the terrace outside my room and watch the drama around me. Mr. Wright claimed the mineral deposits at the base of the hill attracted the lightning. Storms were spectacular.

Today the valley is much the same as in those early years. Winter created an icy wasteland in the valley, and on cold, moonlit nights I could see Mr. and Mrs. Wright's eight-year-old daughter Iovanna's wild, black pony with flying mane racing over the frozen ponds. In spring, the valley became a fairyland of blossoms edging the ponds and drifting up the hills. Once, I asked Mr. Wright if

Taliesin in winter, 1939

one of the fields sweeping up from the valley could be planted in flowers instead of hay, alfalfa, or oats. A practical farmer, he obliged by planting buckwheat. Butterflies and bees hummed over the white blossoms waving in the breeze.

The river valleys are covered with forests of willow, cottonwood, river birch, silver maple, sugar maple, and red maple, with clumps of brilliant cardinal flowers and other surprises on the floor. Cedar glades and forests of aspen, birch, basswood, maple, oak, walnut, butternut hickory, and white and red pine blanket the hillsides. Along the roadsides laden with sumac, gray dogwood, wild berries, ferns, Solomon's seal, bittersweet, and many other fascinating plants, we still find endless decorating possibilities for our rooms. That area of Wisconsin is lush and subtropical in summer. When Indian summer turns into winter most Fellowship members now migrate to our campus in Scottsdale, Arizona.

A few, who stay in Wisconsin year round, still experience the dynamic seasonal changes in the valley. Those of us who return each spring and summer to enjoy its lush beauty can still remember vividly, though, the winters of those early years when Taliesin lay gently sleeping under the white snow while life bustled within its shelter.

Fellows enjoying a Wisconsin spring day in the Taliesin valley

At Etta Hocking's market in Dodgeville before the first trip to Arizona.
Cornelia is standing in the far left in the back row, 1935

Front row (kneeling left to right): Abe Dombar, Iovanna Wright, Jim Thomson; 2nd row: Etta Parsons, Etta's mother, Etta's husband, Bob Mosher
3rd row: Peter Frankel, Mabel Morgan, Bill Bernoudy, Jack Howe, Will Schwanke's wife, Mrs. Wright, Mary Thomson, Hulda Brierly Drake, Alfie Bush
4th row: Cornelia Brierly, Don Thompson, Bud Shaw, Fred Langhorst, Benny Dombar, Will Schwanke, Bob Bishop, Mr. Wright, Betty Barnsdall, Edgar Kaufmann Jr.;
last row: unknown, John Lautner, Edgar Tafel, Mary Bud Lautner, Bruce Richards

TALIESIN FELLOWSHIP HEADS WEST

Because of the severe winter of 1934–35 the whole pattern of Taliesin life began to change. Most of the men spent all of their time sawing wood in the deep snow of the forest by day and feeding logs to the lusty boilers of the house and studio by day and night just to keep us warm.

Mr. Wright made the decision to head for Arizona—exciting news for all of us! Everyone bought sleeping bags— ten dollars for a down bag at Sears—and we began to plan for the necessities that needed to be taken for such a long journey. We loaded the big red Taliesin truck with our home-cured hams and bacon, hundreds of jars of canned vegetables from the garden, vegetables from the root cellar such as squash, carrots, and turnips and barrels of sauerkraut and eggs buried in salt to preserve them.

The day the temperature fell to 40 degrees below zero, Mr. Wright alerted us to be ready to leave by four the next morning. The men silenced the boilers and drained the steam from all radiators. We sat on our luggage that bitter cold morning in January waiting for Mr. Wright and his assistant, Gene Masselink, to return from Madison with Mr. Wright's Cord car.

They appeared about six o'clock, but the Cord couldn't make it up the hill through the deep snow. Gene dragged a mattress down to cover the engine. About four hours later our caravan left: the truck, a station wagon, and several cars, all winding through a canyon of snow plowed into drifts as high as the telephone wires.

Our first stop was Dodgeville where Etta Hocking had invited us for a send-off brunch. For years she had owned a grocery and meat market in Dodgeville and had been a wonderful provider for the Fellowship, trusting Mr. and Mrs. Wright with necessary supplies when they had no money. She welcomed us that morning with a hearty farm brunch and with her usual good cheer sent all twenty-five of us on our way.

During the trip we stayed in low-rate hotels or tourist cabins, sometimes six of us to a room, at a cost of about sixty-five cents each. We drew straws to see who would get the beds, and the others slept in sleeping bags on the floor. Once, in an old frame hotel beside a railroad track, our rooms rumbled with every passing train. Knowing the frugal circumstances of our travels, many of Mr. Wright's friends came to our rescue during the trip. William Allen White, the well-known editor of the *Emporia Gazette,* and his gracious wife entertained us all at a luncheon in their home in Emporia, Kansas. Henry Allen, Governor of Kansas, treated us to dinner in the house that Mr. Wright had designed for him in Wichita.

When we arrived in Tulsa, Mr. Wright's cousin, Richard Lloyd Jones,

Richard Lloyd Jones house. Tulsa, Oklahoma, 1935

Governor Henry Allen's house interior. Wichita, Kansas, 1935

Hacienda at Chandler, Arizona

invited us to spend the night by spreading our sleeping bags throughout his spacious house. All these prominent men joined in lively and fascinating fireside conversations with Mr. Wright. No gathering ever has more spirit than when two powerful Lloyd Jones cousins meet, either in agreement or in conflict!

Being in Richard's house thrilled us all. Its quiet, domestic scale belies photographs that make it appear much larger. Most of the exterior walls are glass that give the interior light a transfiguring opalescence. It is completely different from the Allen house, which Mr. Wright designed during World War I. Being a more northern house, the Allen house walls are of sheltering brick with bands of windows protected under extended eaves. It is a wide, elegant, handsome house, palatial but intimate in scale and quiet in feeling. Richard's house has many of the same qualities, but its complete originality is very exciting.

After the 2,200-mile trip, we finally arrived in Chandler, Arizona where Dr. Chandler, an elderly, distinguished man who had founded the town, greeted us. In the late 1920s Dr. Chandler had commissioned Mr. Wright to design a desert hotel. Mr. Wright envisioned a very original building—using cement block with an abstract design of the saguaro cactus—to be called San-Marcos-in-the-Desert. Just as the drawings were completed, the bottom fell out of the stock market in the

Courtyard of Hacienda. A sleeping bag is left on the lawn

1929 crash. Mr. Wright and Dr. Chandler had become good friends by then, and, at Mr. Wright's request, the doctor offered the use of the Hacienda where the Fellowship could live and work during the spring of 1935.

Chandler was a cattle town with stockyards. A section of little shacks and dusty yards, where the sombreroed Mexican men staged their cock fights, we found most interesting. Dr. Chandler owned the town's San Marcos Resort Hotel inhabited mostly by people in wheelchairs with ear trumpets, or so it seemed to us. Actually, Gene Tunney, the famous prize fighter; President Herbert Hoover; and other notables came and went there. As young, spirited people we apprentices often helped entertain the elderly guests.

The Hacienda where we stayed had formerly been a polo stable where stalls had been converted into single rooms for fruit growers. From the road a two-section wooden gate opened to reveal a broad concrete entry court sheltered by a high roof but open to the lawn and fields beyond. On one side of the entry court there was a large living room and an apartment for Mr. and Mrs. Wright, while the dining area and kitchen stretched out on the other side. From this section of the house two wings built at right angles extended out on either side of the grassy courtyard. Each of these opposite wings had eight apprentice

Working on Broadacre City model in Hacienda Courtyard, 1935
Left to right: (far left group) Bob Mosher, Blaine Drake, Jack Howe, unknown, Cornelia, Mr. Wright, Bob Bishop
(near right group, standing) Mary Bud Lautner, Benny Dombar, Jim Thomson; (sitting) Alfie Bush, Hulda Brierly, Mary Thomson, Bruce Richards

*Cornelia (left) working on
Broadacre City model, 1935*
Will Schwanke (back), Benny Dombar (front)

Gene Masselink working on Broadacre City model, 1935

rooms that opened onto the lawn. On the lawn, Elmer Shoop, the Indian trader, came and spread out blankets and jewelry for all of us to fight over.

Out beyond the courtyard there were fields of sheep and alfalfa. The poor farmer in the adjacent alfalfa field spent all his time filling up gopher holes in order to hoard the precious irrigation water. As a result, the field was a lush, munchable green for his mules to enjoy.

Continuing our work

On the grass and under the roofed-over concrete entrance court we started to build a model of Broadacre City to illustrate Mr. Wright's concept of a plan for decentralization of cities. During the preceding fall in Wisconsin we had fashioned some small individual models of houses. At the same time, Edgar Kaufmann Sr. had come to commission a house (later to become Fallingwater). When Mr. Wright discussed the idea of the model for decentralization of cities with him, Mr. Kaufmann offered to finance it, thus making the Fellowship trip to Arizona possible.

We constructed the 12-foot-square Broadacre City model in four sections, with each plywood section representing a square mile. Contours made of layered plywood were added to one section to form a hill, giving diversity to the landscape. When the base was in place, Mr. Wright assigned us individual plots to develop.

We needed an overall color scheme. Both Mr. and Mrs. Wright liked the plot that I had colored in earth tones, and this became the accepted color scheme for the entire model. Using former plans that Mr. Wright had developed for houses and buildings, the apprentices fabricated many miniature jewel-like models for the large Broadacre model. It also included conventional-sized models of St. Marks Tower (an early skyscraper design, which Mr. Wright later developed as the Price Tower in Bartlesville, Oklahoma); a farm unit; and small houses that would be compatible with the Depression-era economy.

We were in the sun, we were young, and we were having a wonderful time in spite of the fact that our food supply from Wisconsin had dwindled, limiting us much of the time to peanut butter, salt pork, and sauerkraut. In the early mornings about six o'clock, we came bounding out of our doors, greeting one another across the grassy courtyard, ready for a new day and a new experience.

Not all young apprentices that made the trip west returned to Wisconsin. The trip was full of many new experiences to divert young minds. Fred Langhorst

The model as a concept in progress, 1935

(Left to right around the model): Burt Goodrich, Edgar Kaufmann Jr., Blaine Drake, Benny Dombar, Abe Dombar, John Lautner, Jim Thomson, Edgar Tafel, Alfie Bush, Bruce Richards, Jack Howe, Karl Monrad, Mr. Wright, Will Schwanke, Gene Masselink, Bob Bishop, Bill Bernoudy.

Cornelia with the St. Marks Tower model as part of the Broadacre installation, Summer 1935

joined the Fellowship in 1933. During harvest time in Wisconsin with most of us fully occupied shocking corn, Fred made an impressive mask of colored corn kernels and also a handsome stone sculpture. His many talents included a keen enjoyment of gathering local tales from old timers. When we drove west on our trip to Arizona, Fred lagged behind the caravan. A garrulous fellow, he stopped along the way to talk to Native American Indians, cowboys, gas station attendants, and trading post characters. He bargained for a substantial number of old Indian rugs, baskets, turquoise pawn bracelets, and belt buckles. When Fred arrived at Chandler, with a loaded van, he wore a ten-gallon hat, cowboy chaps, silver-studded boots, and Indian jewelry. He had turned from an Illinois Mark Twain buff to a dedicated westerner.

Fred stayed up late at night reading western lore. Getting up at six in the morning was not part of his schedule. At about ten or eleven o'clock Mr. Wright would miss him and say, "Where's Fred? Go wake him!" Finally, one morning Mr. Wright had him wakened and called into the office. He said, "Fred, you're wasting your time here." Fred's surprising reaction was one of fury. He said, "For Christ's sake, Mr. Wright, why didn't you tell me that months ago?" So Fred took his ten-gallon hat, his guns, his chaps, his newly acquired bundle of Indian rugs, and his dog, and left for a sleepier lair.

Time for play

We had many picnics to explore the desert, one at the site of Ocotilla Camp. This camp, built by Mr. Wright for the group of people helping him make drawings for San Marcos-in-the-Desert, had an unusual design of wood and canvas that gave the extraordinary sense of ships sailing in the desert. Mr. Wright built it, lived in it, and abandoned it after three months because The Crash made building the hotel impossible. By the time we arrived to picnic there, Indians had plundered and carried away most of the camp.

We had overnight excursions to the Superstition Mountains. Sometimes we followed the Mexicans up the washes as they panned for gold. A day's work yielded a small bottle of gold dust, worth about $2.50. This, during the Depression, afforded an adequate wage to keep a man in beans and coffee and feed his burro. At night we joined the hospitable Mexicans at their fires. They always offered us beans and mighty powerful boiled coffee.

One dry season we were sleeping in a wash at the base of the Superstition Mountains when a flash flood swept over us in the middle of the night. We crawled out of our soggy sleeping bags and ended the night sitting in the cars, wrapped in blankets and coats.

We usually carried grapefruit to quench our thirst. Once we left some on a rock at the base of the Superstitions while we climbed to a high ledge, high enough that the grapefruit appeared as yellow dots. When complaining about our thirst and wishing we'd carried the grapefruit, we looked down and saw others of the group spy our fruit. With parched throats we watched them peel and enjoy our thirst quenchers.

Taking leave

As spring came, our thoughts began to turn to Taliesin and the farming and gardening that awaited us. Taking our leave of Dr. Chandler, we rounded up the caravan of cars and once again packed for the long journey back home.

Some of us, riding in the Cord, headed for the Apache Trail, a rutted and treacherous wagon trail in the wilderness about thirty miles east of Phoenix. Along the trail the car broke down. We sat in the blazing sun all day, waiting for Gene

Masselink who had walked miles to get help. He finally met a farmer who brought him back and fixed the offending carburetor. We managed that night to get to Pine, Arizona, where five of us shared a lone tourist cabin. The next day we broke down in Oak Creek Canyon, and so forth, throughout the whole trip.

When we got to Iowa, things seemed to be going smoothly, so we debated detouring to see Mr. Wright's Willey House in Minneapolis. Just then, we heard the crunch, crunch, crunch of the wire wheels breaking. So, as fast as possible in such a precarious situation, we limped on to Wisconsin where we met a glorious spring, with blossoms of wild crab apples and lilacs, and all the myriad shades of green that seemed incredible after the intense heat and dryness of the desert. We arrived home at last. Taliesin embraced us with its peaceful buildings and courtyards.

Tuweep

The next winter we traveled to Arizona, staying again at the Hacienda, but working on projects other than Broadacre City. Everyone who went on the Fellowship caravan from Chandler, Arizona, to Wisconsin in the spring of 1936 has a different story to tell. Mine

Packing the red stake truck at Hacienda, 1935
Left to right: Blaine Drake, Bob Mosher, Hulda Drake

happened to be colored by an excruciatingly painful case of sciatica.

Before we left Chandler, my friend Edgar Tafel suggested that I could get help from his masseur. He took me to the labyrinth of dark halls in the basement of the Adams Hotel in Phoenix. There, saying he'd return shortly, he abandoned me in a space curtained off with bed sheets. Soon a burly, muscular man stripped to the waist, displaying his totally tattooed torso, confronted me. Handing me a towel he said, "Here's your fig leaf, dearie."

Filled with pain and apprehension and too miserable to leave, I showered. Then, putting me on the couch, he saturated me with oil, manipulated me toe-by-toe and pummeled me muscle-by-muscle. Mr. X gave a running dialogue as he displayed the tattooed butterfly that opened and shut at his elbow, the mermaid that appeared to swim, the angel whose wings moved as he flexed his back muscles, a peacock on his chest, initialed bleeding hearts concealed under one arm, monsters of the sea, and many other works of the tattooer's art. Subtly, his manipulations began to change to caresses. "You have beautiful eyes," he said. I felt terribly weak and my only thought was escape.

Edgar burst in. "Ready?"

"Not yet," the bruiser said.

"Be back later," Edgar said as he dashed out.

"Edgar, Edgar, don't leave!" I cried, but he had gone. Dragging myself from the couch, feeling completely defeated and full of pain, I dressed to escape as quickly as I could. When I got to the street, Edgar was nowhere to be seen. Standing on the street corner, balancing from one aching leg to the other and trying to forget my plight, I spent a miserable hour waiting for him. The only people around were cowboys hitching their horses as they came in for a night on the town. They stood around joshing one another and comparing silver studded saddles and boots. By the time Edgar arrived, I felt too ill to complain.

Caravan adventure

The next day our caravan, four cars, and the stake truck loaded with equipment and food, took off. Packing the truck became a traumatic experience. During the stay in Chandler, everyone had acquired more possessions—Indian blankets, baskets, and other souvenirs. The boys packing the truck ran out of space. Confronted with the situation, Mr. Wright, general that he was, boarded the truck and systematically emptied everyone's boxes and suitcases, tucking the contents into the interstices. We stood in disbelief, dismay, and frustration. The rest of the gear was crammed into the truck, readying it for the road.

The next morning we started on our way to the Grand Canyon, going through Arizona's scenic red rock and juniper country around Sedona and Oak Creek. At our first camping spot on the rim of the canyon, we spread our sleeping bags. In the morning we woke up under a blanket of snow. While cooking breakfast, we had a glorious view of the sunrise flooding the canyon with changing patterns of light and shadow that spotlighted buttes, pinnacles, and rock castles of awesome dimensions. Architecture of the Master Builder!

From his boyhood Mr. Wright remembered the excitement of a gold rush somewhere in the High Sierras. Studying the map, he spotted the town of Goldfield. It became our next destination. On the way, we pitched camp on a dry lake bed in Death Valley. During the night a sandstorm came up. The blowing sand swept into our sleeping bags, into our hair, ears, eyes, and noses. Lying on the cold, uneven ground, I felt excruciating pain from my sciatica, and the wind and sand made things worse.

*Kay Schneider (Rattenbury), Noverre Musson, Benny Dombar, and Jack Howe
ready for the trip back to Taliesin, Wisconsin, 1936*

By rolling in my sleeping bag bundle, I managed to take shelter in the back of a car, but even so, the wind piled sand into every accessible opening. Since we dressed and undressed in the sleeping bags, we kept our clothes with us, which meant that before we crawled out in the morning, we had to pull on clothes full of sand. Once up, everyone busied himself shaking out sleeping bags and clothes. After eating breakfast—eggs and bacon "true grit style"—we packed up and started climbing to the snow-capped Sierras.

Goldfield sat on a high, grassy plain. Tall grass had settled in around the abandoned houses and decaying buildings. Several low houses, half buried in grass, had walls and windows made of green and lavender bottles aged by the sun. A Victorian hotel survived, inhabited by a few old miners, true believers who really thought they would sometime make a strike. The lobby had circular high-backed, red velour seats for which sitting space had once gone for $100 a night. The proprietress, a voluptuous blond, wore a gold chain belt from which hung a clutch of gold keys about eight or twelve inches long. The rest of the town seemed totally abandoned, although it must have had a post office since the name appeared on the map. Recently,

Goldfield's mining past has led it to become a tourist town in the High Sierras of western Nevada.

Having satisfied this youthful dream, Mr. Wright decided our next destination would be through Zion National Park and Bryce Canyon. So, back to Las Vegas and on to the parks. In Bryce Canyon, Mr. Wright talked to a ranger who bragged that one could best see the Grand Canyon from the North Rim at Tuweep. Back we trekked to Las Vegas and on to Tuweep.

Finding the trail

Our car fell behind the others, and as it went up a steep mountain road, we weren't at all sure we trailed the other cars. We met a farmer with his team and hay wagon. "Have you seen any people drive up this road?" Shifting his tobacco to the other cheek, he drawled, "Lord, yes, the whole east just passed!" So we knew the others had gone ahead on their way to Tuweep, even though this narrow dirt road didn't seem like a much-traveled trail.

Our car had lost time because we had to jam four of us in a small Ford with a rumble seat full of luggage. Driving through Bryce Canyon, we didn't notice that a bag had flown off. When we

missed it, we retraced our steps and, sure enough, found it in the middle of the highway.

Gene Masselink, Edgar Tafel, and I rode in the front seat, and Bob Mosher insisted on flailing around on top of the luggage in the rumble seat. When we arrived on a high plateau, it had turned so cold that our faces were chapped and our lips were cracked. When I resorted to lipstick, the men said, "Give us some." Not fussy about outlines, they smeared it liberally over their faces. About that time, we came to the town of Short Creek, a desolate looking settlement of weathered, unpainted houses set in dusty yards, and one small store with a hand-written, cockeyed wooden sign saying, "Uncle Joe's."

As the men tried to wipe their faces clean, the lipstick only smeared more. Famished, we went into the store anyway, only to find their total stock consisted of one can of tomato juice. We asked where we could get sandwiches. Uncle Joe directed us to one of the larger houses where we found five or six women, raggedly dressed, most of them carrying babies. Hesitatingly, they said they thought they could give us egg sandwiches. "Okay, fine," we said.

Outside, we could see a young fellow with a horse. He leaped on the horse,

Camping in the dry lake bed in Death Valley

rode through the dust to a house, banged on the door, then rode to the next house. A man with a small movie camera on a tripod continued to crank a film of this would-be Paul Revere. After a considerable wait, it began to get dark, and we became anxious about finding our group. "Are the sandwiches ready?" The embarrassed women said, "Someone is out in the town trying to find butter."

"We don't need butter," we said, thereby clearing the way for thick, sour bread sandwiches. Paying and thanking them, we went on, but the road turned into a trail of matted grass, and as the light dimmed, we had to get out with a flashlight to detect signs of the other cars. Finally, we came to a dead end with boulders and fallen logs across our path. Off in the distance, we could see a faint light and decided to aim for it. Light beamed from a log cabin set in a yard where steers wallowed in the dust. Gene went to the door. When a little lady opened it, Gene said, "Can you tell us how to get to Tuweep?"

"This," she said sweetly, "is Tuweep. Won't you come in?" We were all shocked as we still thought we would find a town where we could get food and gas. The lady insisted on giving us coffee as she explained that she was the postmistress for the cowboys in that area. Once every two weeks a postman delivered mail to Tuweep from a station 96 miles away. Three years before, the cabin had burned. Her husband, who traveled out on the range, must have returned regularly, as she had three babies (all under three years) sleeping in homemade cradles by windows covered with skins.

Our newfound friend, once a librarian, had opted for this life on the range where cattle and wild horses ruled. Delighted to have people to talk to, she kept urging another cup of coffee, but we were anxious to join the others. When we asked for directions to the Canyon rim, she drew a map of a certain tree, a group of boulders, etc. With her accurate descriptions, we finally saw the bonfire that our people had made to guide us.

The next morning we awoke to the magnificence of a canyon sunrise, only to discover that we had placed some of our sleeping bags perilously close to the edge. Mabel Morgan had already started a fire to cook what little food remained. Some people tried to gather water for coffee from small pools among the rocks, but every time they found a likely pool, Mrs. Wright's two wolfhounds plunged in and thwarted their efforts. The wolfhounds, Sasha and Dushan, were beautiful but dumb. Later when we camped by a freezing lake, they plunged in, stood there shivering, but couldn't get out. Wading in to rescue them didn't help as later they both got distemper. Since no kennel would keep them, apprentice Everett Baker had to nurse them in a motel until they could travel. We had "breakfast" at Tuweep without coffee and scant fare. Each car's passengers had their own adventure story to tell of "getting to Tuweep."

Troubles along the trail

At one point, Betty Barnsdall (seventeen-year-old daughter of Aline Barnsdall for whom Mr. Wright built the Hollyhock House) who had been driving her new La Salle over the rocks, stopped, went to Mr. Wright's car, flung open the door and said, "God damn you, Mr. Wright, I'm not going any further." Mr. Wright became furious, but Mrs. Wright scolded Betty and managed to soothe all frayed nerves. And the caravan continued.

Along the way we managed to dip up water for the cars. Getting sufficient gas to keep going remained a bit more difficult. Each car contributed enough gas to a lead car to make the eighty miles to a filling station. As we waited a herd of wild horses galloped across the plain as we moved over the high plateau. The lead car eventually arrived with cans of gas for all the cars, which by that time had stalled at intervals along the way.

Years later, we saw a magazine article about a government raid on the last polygamist town of Short Creek. The photo showed the leader of the community with his multiple wives and children—the same wives that had given us sandwiches. The authorities had spied on them by pretending to make a movie of Paul Revere and they caught the poor leader and sent him to jail. An unhappy ending for a family who, in spite of their poverty, had done everything they could to help us.

Taliesin valley under the blanket of winter, 1939

THE TWO TALIESINS

Legacy of the Land

Every spring and fall as we travel from the site of one Taliesin to the other, we are always surprised by the contrasts of our two environments. When we leave the desert in late spring, the intensity of the sun has usually burned the low sage-green foliage to a crisp and divested the trees of their minuscule leaves. Heat radiates from the parched desert floor and from the volcanic rocks of the mountain. Desert dust devils swirl through the air carrying tents and umbrellas aloft.

When we arrive in Wisconsin, our moist valley cradles us in the all-pervasive green of lush forests and meadows. This subtropical atmosphere gives no hint of severe winters to come. But Taliesin, with its golden limestone masonry and plaster the color of river sand, has gently sloping roofs and broad sheltering eaves that lend a sense of security when winter arrives, creating a crystalline wonderland. During the late '30s and early '40s, when snow glistened on the roofs and icicles hung from the low eaves to the ground, two peacocks (a gift to Mr. Wright from a friend), spread their brilliant, iridescent tail feathers over the cascade of icicles. This gorgeous spectacle confirmed Mr. Wright's often expressed belief that "exuberance is beauty."

For Mr. Wright, the selection of the two Taliesin sites proved vitally important. By their character he established a grammar for the buildings that in turn formulated a lifestyle for his family and the Fellowship. His buildings and sites enhanced one another by preserving the native character of the landscape. Mr. Wright's approach to architecture and landscaping and their effect on people's lives can best be understood by the choice of sites for the two Taliesins.

On a hill overlooking a pond, the Wisconsin River, the forested hills, and the valley farms of his ancestors, Mr. Wright established Taliesin at Spring Green. Using local stone and river sand, the buildings arose as a testament to ancient seas and as a natural circumstance in league with forests of hemlock, pine, oak, maple, walnut, hickory, and other varieties.

Taliesin lies in the southern part of the Driftless Area of Wisconsin—a geologically historic land-island the size of Denmark. Three different ages of glaciers, with ice sometimes two-miles thick, approached this area and deposited their end moraines around its perimeters but never encroached on its deep virgin soil or its ancient forests. In tertiary times these lush forests encircled the globe, but now only three remnants remain— one in this Driftless Area, another in the Appalachians, and the third in a remote area of southeastern China.

Since the Driftless Area is a unique area in the world, it serves as a benchmark for study by global scientists. As the glaciers receded, the outwash flowed through the broad valleys of the Driftless Area and swirled around its picturesque sandstone and limestone cliffs, leaving forests and prairies intact with deep productive soil. Because Taliesin enjoys the legacy of this beautiful driftless area

Construction of the Hillside drafting room at Taliesin in Spring Green

with its deep rich deposits of top soil, our gardens and farm flourish.

As the house encircles the forested hill it adjusts to changing contours and elevations. The entrance stairs, terminating in the slopes of the hill, are banked by native ferns, vines, high bush cranberries, and cow parsnips. Although the gardens are laid out in geometric beds, the natural drift of the foliage gives an informal feeling to the asymmetric plan.

At the entry, Mrs. Wright and her young daughters, Svetlana and Iovanna, planted a clump of three gray birches that now shade a bed of ferns, spleenwort,

maidenhair ferns, and Solomon Seal. Courtyard flower beds are also planted with native bee balm, phlox, butterfly weed, tiger lilies, tall bluebells, and sweet rocket. Mr. Wright's landscaping vision went beyond the immediate environs of the house to encompass the entire panorama of hills and valleys. Mr. Wright designed lines of the roofs, eaves, garden walls, and terraces to extend the vision to infinity. When rundown farm buildings marred the scenery, Mr. Wright bought the land and took away the offending houses, barns, silos, and sheds. Then, with the help of eager

apprentices, he landscaped the valley with native trees and shrubs and rebuilt the dam to enlarge the pond.

When he had the farm buildings torn down, it shocked local people by what to them was wasteful, but Mr. Wright—like Emerson—felt that "Beauty is its own excuse for being." Mr. Wright considered "beauty the highest form of morality." Besides his interest in beautifying the landscape, he encouraged everyone to look neat when working, colorful at picnics, and elegant at formal evenings.

To beautify the fields and to prevent soil erosion, Mr. Wright was the first to contour the fields in graceful, curving bands of planting that the University of Wisconsin sent students to study. In the 1985 book, *The Crowning of the American Landscape: Eight Great Spaces and their Buildings* (Princeton University Press, 1985), Walter L. Creese lists our valley as one of the eight most beautiful in the United States.

When the golden and red leaves of Indian summer begin to drift through autumn sunshine, they mark the time to start our trek to Arizona. We leave behind a few stalwart men who enjoy the challenge of severe winters. They stay to maintain our architectural office and take care of Taliesin in the long Wisconsin winter.

Taliesin West desert evening. Triangular pool under construction in foreground

Arriving at Taliesin West, we enter a totally different world of endless space. Taliesin rests near the northern limit of the Great Sonoran Desert, which extends south through Sonora, Mexico, west to the Colorado River basin, and east into southeastern New Mexico. The great masonry masses of our buildings arise from the gently sloping Maricopa Mesa at the foot of the McDowell Mountains. The spacious light-drenched rooms open out to extensive stands of prickly cactus and sharp boulder-strewn mountains. The desert, which at first may seem desolate, teems with plant, animal, and bird life, which over the centuries have adapted for survival. Their simple adaptations create fascinating structural patterns studied by our architectural apprentices for the creation of buildings and abstract designs.

When moisture is plentiful, the desert and mountains become a luxuriant garden. In spring, yellow daisy-like flowers of brittlebush bloom profusely. All across the desert palo verde trees glow with ethereal yellow blossoms. Around the curve of the mountain a golden poppy field is interspersed with blue lupine and wild onion. Some cacti, like the saguaro, are unique to our area of the Sonoran Desert, but the extended cactus family is indigenous to North and South America. A dry spring creates a dormant condition for most plants. But when the flowers flourish in the spring, so do the birds, as endless migrations stop to enjoy our oasis.

We first built Taliesin West in the midst of virgin plants—saguaro, prickly pear, cholla, and staghorn cactus. We lived among all the animals, many of which have retreated to the hills. Wild horses that eluded the barbed wire corrals of the American Indians brushed against our tents. In summer the mountain lions came to drink at our pools and families of javelinas traveled single file through the washes hunting their favorite food—prickly pear.

Typical early tent construction
Left to right: Brandoch Peters, Aubrey Banks

Living in tents kept us close to desert life. At night we checked our tents for rattlesnakes and our sleeping bags for scorpions, kissing bugs, or black widow spiders. Often we encountered packrats, skunks, ring-tailed cats, rock squirrels, and deer. Sometimes in the dark we would bump into a wild burro. After a rain we enjoyed the fresh smell of creosote bush as we explored local canyons and mountains. Our apprentices still have the opportunity to live in tents close to this diverse and inspiring life, as the Taliesin West campus comprises many acres of virgin desert.

Coyotes still come to the Taliesin gardens to feast on pyracantha berries, and javelina drink at outlying pools and root up our plants. Deer thrive on vegetable gardens. Rabbits nibble our lawn. In the hot summer they lie spread-eagle in the dirt under the shade trees. Displaced by houses, jackrabbits and roadrunners, which used to live among the creosote bushes in the valley, have taken sanctuary with us.

Our buildings with their sloping masonry recall the angles of the mountains. They are built with sand hauled from the washes and with an unusual red quartzite that only occurs on the one mountain above the campus. Geologists have officially designated this hard red rock, spewed from some ancient inferno, as "Taliesin Quartzite."

In clearing the building site, Mr. Wright saved all cactus to landscape the grounds. Taken from the context of the natural desert, these barbed, spiny cacti eventually created a hostile environment around the buildings. Visitors were constantly impaled on spines. Eventually, Mr. Wright replaced all cactus with tropical foliage. He planted exotic bougainvillea, red-berried pyracantha, and flowering oleander within the footprint of the buildings. He extended garden walls and gravel terraces to tie the plan of the buildings to the desert beyond, to give breadth to the entire scheme, and to conserve water by eliminating large planting areas. Mr. Wright left everything beyond the garden walls with all its original growth. The desert trees, palo verde, ironwood, and mesquite, are all legumes—nature's way of using plants that develop virgin soil by the nitrogen-fixing bacteria on their roots.

When we started building in 1937, the entire valley north of Camelback Road in modern day Phoenix was open range. Local herders drove hundreds of thousands of sheep through the valley as they went back and forth from winter pastures to summer fields on Arizona's Mogollon Rim. At night we saw the herders' fires, heard the bleating sheep, the howling coyotes, and the barking sheep dogs.

In early years Brahmin cattle roamed through the valley eating the scant tufts of grass; desert grasses, low to the ground, quickly develop nutritious seeds browsed by cattle. One dry summer during World War II when our buildings were not yet enclosed, a starved cow wandered into the open kitchen and ate my sister's ration books. The story made the Phoenix paper as the best excuse given to the Ration Board for replacement coupons.

We all liked to go to town to gather local folklore in Scottsdale—a dusty crossroads—a real western town with cowboys and an impressive sheriff who wore a handlebar mustache, a large Stetson hat, and a revolver in his gun belt. He epitomized the legendary, honest, no-nonsense sheriff. He had clout with all the people while enforcing the law and settling disputes on the spot. When a drunken fellow brawling in the saloon went after the sheriff with a chair, the sheriff pulled his gun and shot him. Our boys couldn't wait to get to town the next morning for the inquest, held on the unpaved, dusty street in front of the saloon. When town elders asked the sheriff why he shot the fellow, he said, "He was a comin' at me with a chair. It was either a matter of runnin' or shootin', and it ain't befittin' the law to run." He was acquitted on the spot.

What started out during the Depression as a rough sketch for a Taliesin winter camp has grown into a permanent group of buildings constructed by apprentices from all over the world. Taliesin West, like Taliesin in Wisconsin, enjoys the legacy of a very special site that nature has been preparing for countless ages. In two totally different environments we have developed multifaceted lifestyles of work and play.

Dark Days

In November 1936, when we heard that Mr. Wright had pneumonia, we were all in a state of shock. Taliesin was suddenly blanketed with a hush of concern. Mrs. Wright called a prominent doctor from Madison. He advised her to take Mr. Wright to the hospital immediately. This suggestion unnerved Mrs. Wright who knew Mr. Wright would have strenuous objections.

Dr. Wahl from Spring Green advised against it. A rough country doctor, he had pulled many patients through such crises by nursing them at home. We apprentices, all very young, had little experience, and, with such a critical decision to make, Mrs. Wright longed to consult a more mature person. Carl Sandburg arrived just at that anxious time. In the stress of the situation we had forgotten he was invited for the weekend. Mrs. Wright asked his advice. Frowning in thought, he paced back and forth, rubbing his hands through his white hair. Suddenly he stopped short with a pontifical pronouncement, "A decision must be made!" With that he walked out of the room. Astounded and disgusted, Mrs. Wright never forgave him. It seemed he had less interest in Mr. Wright's serious illness than the disruption of his weekend.

With Dr. Wahl's help, Mrs. Wright decided to keep Mr. Wright at home. Bob Mosher, Gene Masselink, and others did round-the-clock duties to nurse Mr. Wright and keep fires going in his room.

Egotist Carl Sandburg insisted on performing for the Fellowship. We reluctantly gathered in the dining room. "I've just written this little story," he said, "Cornelia, you have a good voice, you can read it aloud." It was a nonsense tale. I can't remember it exactly, but the superciliousness of it against the somber atmosphere among us remains with me. Although I'm not quoting it exactly, the gist of it goes something like this: "In the sloom of the slimdidge the gloogs do what they want to do. They have knot holes in their heads. Put your fingers in."

In despair over Mr. Wright's condition, Mrs. Wright called her old mentor Mr. Gurdjieff. He gave her advice on how to nurse Mr. Wright and on how she should take care of herself, as he knew her well enough to know she would completely neglect herself for Mr. Wright. At his suggestion, once a day she went for a walk in the brisk fall air and lived mostly on milk, orange juice, and raw cabbage. Her daughter Svetlana, (who Mr. Wright had adopted), Kay Schneider, my sister Hulda, and I helped prepare things in the kitchen and furnished the needs of the trained nurse.

With Mrs. Wright's constant vigilance and Dr. Wahl's common sense advice, Mr. Wright finally passed through the crisis. When he started to talk about wanting "a big red India rubber ball," everyone thought he was delirious. But no, he just remembered a poem by A. A. Milne that he had read to Iovanna, his little daughter. It's about King John who, "was not a good man," who pleaded with Father Christmas, "Bring me a big red India rubber ball!"

Mr. Wright asked to smell a fresh apple and wished for a fresh papaya, something never heard of in Spring Green, Wisconsin. So someone drove 200 miles to buy one in the Chicago produce market. Mr. Gurdjieff suggested a recipe for a nourishing calf's head soup, which we girls made fresh daily when Mr. Wright started to recuperate.

As he gathered strength, Mrs. Wright began to plan for the future. As soon as he could travel, they took the train to Phoenix, Arizona, where he could rest and get well at Jokake Inn.

From there in the spring of 1937, Mr. Wright ventured into the desert by the McDowell Mountains and bought the tract of land on which we started to build Taliesin West that very fall.

Our first shelter

The fall of 1937 marked our first season on Maricopa Mesa, the site of Taliesin West. This grand experiment and adventure energized Mr. and Mrs. Wright and all of us. Having arrived with sleeping bags, we piled our equipment on the

high ledge of the first wash and immediately started to build a lean-to. One end served as kitchen, with a two-burner kerosene stove and a long dining table made of rough planks. The other end held a drawing board, our clothes, and other small possessions.

At night, until we built shelters, we spread out over the desert with sleeping bags. Mr. Wright tried an experiment of having the men build shelters of two-by-fours and chicken wire covered with sisalcraft, a roofing paper. Apprentices Burt Goodrich and Manuel Sandoval, both master craftsmen, started a three-sided shelter with a shed roof for themselves. It had room for two cots with a wardrobe between. With this shelter partially built, Mr. Wright took all the boys to lay out the camp, so Mildred Daley and I were given the task of finishing the shelter for ourselves. Mildred came from Oconomowoc, Wisconsin, but stayed for only a season.

Neither of us had ever used a hammer or saw, but we plunged into the adventure. Sometimes we sawed a two-by-four a little too short. No matter! We attached it with ten-penny nails. Sometimes, the next piece was too long. No matter! We just wedged it in, but in so doing, the first piece was apt to fall out. Finally we got the place together

Traveling to the site of Taliesin West in the red stake truck, turning off the grassy track of Shea Boulevard, 1937

First lean-to kitchen built in a wash
(Cornelia is in the foreground)

End of the lean-to

Mr. Wright and Gene Masselink's first Taliesin West office

with framing, chicken wire, and roofing paper. Pleased with our accomplishment, we enjoyed its shade and protection. Then, one night, a mighty storm swept up from the valley. The rain on the sisal-craft was deafening as was the wild wind. Suddenly, a great gust ripped off our roof, sending a fifteen-foot-long piece of paper whipping back and forth, overhead. Drenched and stunned by the chilling wind, we managed to find a ladder; but capturing the flying roofing defeated us, and we had to head for the lean-to.

Building Taliesin West

Regardless of frugal and sometimes nonexistent finances, Mr. Wright forged ahead with the building of Taliesin West. He organized several crews, one to make the roads, one to survey, and one to level the site. Making the road meant removing the most offensive boulders and leaving smaller stones to be dealt with later. The main thrust and hardest task turned out to be preparing the site, a difficult job because of cactus, rocks, and caliche—a cement-like aggregate that is found in the desert. Since buying equipment was out of the question, pick and shovel and sweat of brow triumphed. We built a temporary office, a shed about the size of an old time privy, for Mr. Wright and his secretary, Gene. In the lean-to, Jack Howe had a drafting board where

Gene Masselink with "champion" cement mixer building Taliesin West

Building Taliesin West studio

he translated Mr. Wright's sketches onto the only affordable paper—brown meat-wrapping paper.

Mr. Wright built the first permanent structure of stone as a vault for the safe-keeping of drawings. Crews hauled rocks from our mountains and sand from the washes with which they formed desert masonry. A small concrete mixer came to do heroic duty. Over the years this same mixer has made concrete for the entire building complex. Although still operating after fifty years, the company that made it recently agreed to replace it, providing the old grizzled performer could be kept as an historic artifact.

While the site work continued, the Fellowship paused to take a trip up the Apache Trail to Roosevelt Dam. On the way we stopped for a boat ride on Apache Lake.

Mr. Wright pointed out the horizontal lines that ran along the cliffs. Being receptive to ideas from nature, he deter-

Ruth Hyland working in the unfinished open kitchen at Taliesin West

Unfinished dining room (Mr. Wright at the head of the table, Mrs. Wright in the hat)

mined to make horizontal lines in the desert masonry at camp.

Desert masonry is laid up in plywood forms. It requires considerable artistry to remember how each rock has been placed in order to make an attractive wall. Placing heavy desert rocks and sometimes getting them up perilously steep, makeshift wobbly plank ramps turned out to be a monumental task. Apprentices took great care to find the right stones for the forms. Our high-spirited Wes (William Wesley Peters), who headed the crew, usually selected the biggest, most heroic-sized rock. In the fall of 1987 at a Fellowship reunion at Taliesin West celebrating the 50th anniversary of the building of these buildings, many former apprentices proudly sought out "that special rock" that they had placed.

After building the vault, the stone piers and fireplace mass of the drafting room grew up from the rubble base. When the finished floor of the drafting room spread out before us, we stood on the broad expanse of concrete, and thrilled with the feeling that we had really arrived. It was the first solid floor underfoot in our desert life. It represented an amazing accomplishment after months of hard labor.

Once the men had finished the drafting room floor, they hoisted redwood beams to receive ceiling panels. Mr. Wright devised a system of canvas-covered frames to act as "shingles." We girls, sitting in the sun, tacked canvas to the frames for roof panels and for operating flaps that enclosed window areas. At that time canvas could be bought inexpensively. It is a breathing material that transmits a diffused light. Tacking canvas became our endless yearly job, not only for construction underway but for replacing the badly weathered flaps, as canvas does not wear long in the desert. The inexpensive redwood and canvas became expedient materials that covered a lot of territory in laying out the grand scheme of Taliesin West. In the intervening years, the redwood, which cracks badly in the dry desert, has been mostly replaced by steel. Glass has been substituted for window areas, and roofs have been made more permanent by using translucent plastic panels for the roof, with canvas panels below in the interiors.

Our first permanent living area was a stone-enclosed room called a "kiva" by Mr. Wright. Since it had a door, however, we didn't have to climb down from the ceiling as the Hopis do in their kivas. With its generous fireplace, this room became a haven in cold, stormy weather. Its stepped up wooden seats made it useful as a small cinema theatre as well as a place where we could serve dinner to our many guests.

During World War II many movie companies came to the valley, and Mr. Wright invited some of the stars to join us for dinner in the Kiva. One night my husband Peter sat next to Jean Arthur. He had problems trying to roll his own wartime cigarette when Jean whipped out a gold case full of real cigarettes. She lit one for herself, closed the case and, as she watched Peter struggling with his, said, "You're having difficulty because you don't have enough stickem in your spit." Peter was furious.

Eventually a new, larger cinema-cabaret took the place of the Kiva, which has become a conference and exhibition room.

Desert floods

Most deserts in western United States get very little rain. Some get none at all, but those that do usually get rain during just one season—either in winter or summer. Our desert, known as the Sonoran, has a different pattern. We receive both winter and summer rains. In winter, winds from the north and northwest bring moisture, and in the summer thunderstorms sweep up from Mexico. Both seasons can bring deluges that cause flash floods. Before the summer thunderstorms come, the desert pulsates with heat waves and desert dust devils whirl over Taliesin. Because of the hard, baked surface of the desert, runoff from sudden rains flows swiftly over the ground causing unexpected cascades of water to hurtle down dry washes and flood the valley.

When we first came, the desert was open range with no impediments to stop the flow of water. During one particularly heavy storm the entire valley flooded for three days from one end to the other. Any attempt to get to Scottsdale ended in disaster for the cars. As soon as the cars hit this wall of water, fanbelts broke and engines stalled. The water swept Fellowship member Dick Carney's car down a swirling wash. Luckily, he managed to crawl out the window and cling to a thorny palo verde tree.

Another time, Johnny Hill and I thought we could get to town in a Bantam roadster even though it had started to rain. We got along fairly well, going west on a narrow, rutted, muddy road known as Shea Boulevard, then south past the Turkey Farm and east on Indian Bend Wash. There we met deep water. Johnny stripped down to his boxer shorts and waded in to test the depth. With such high water we couldn't risk crossing and sat in the car hoping for help. A truckload of local sheepherders came by in a very high truck. Without even glancing at us, they plowed through the wash. There we sat, astonished and frustrated.

A carload of our boys arrived from Taliesin. Since none of us could cross the wash, they walked back to the Turkey Ranch for help. Soon a big loose-jointed, wooden-sided truck came clattering down the road with such speed that water and mud were splashing up all around it, soaking our boys as they desperately clung to the wooden frame. Using rope, the girl driving the truck pulled us all through the gushing water. She apologized for her speed saying, "Sorry, I gotta drive at least 55 miles an hour because of the hayseeds in the carburetor."

One Christmas around 1940 Gene Masselink's parents came to visit. Rowan Maiden went to get them at the train. He borrowed Johnny Hill's new tweed suit and set off in great style with the station wagon. Before he got back it started to rain. Water flowed swiftly over the valley floor but being a newcomer to the desert he thought he could get the Masselinks back to camp faster by leaving the road and driving in a beeline to camp. The car soon stuck in the soft silt with water up to the running boards. Rowan plunged into the flood and by wading and swimming finally arrived in complete exhaustion at camp to ask for help.

All night long our boys went out on search parties, swimming in the icy water, but they could not find the Masselinks. By afternoon the next day the water began to recede. Mr. Wright said, "Boys, I'll find the Masselinks. Get my Lincoln. Some of you ride inside, some on the hood and the rest on the running board. With enough weight we may have traction to get through the mud."

The car started across the desert. Those left at camp gathered on the prow of the Sunset Terrace to watch the red car as it streaked across the desert making a silvery path of splashing water. Mr. Wright and the boys found Dr. and Mrs. Masselink huddled under newspapers to keep from freezing. They had been stranded for almost thirty hours without food, water, or warm clothes. They had come from Michigan with lightweight clothes, prepared to bask in the warm sun of Arizona. Mrs. Masselink later confided to me that just before she left home her doctor had informed her that she had serious heart trouble. He warned her never to get into a stressful situation!

Finished main buildings, 1939

The valley still floods but not so extensively as those in earlier times. Thousands of houses now replace the legions of sheep that once grazed the short clumps of grass growing among the creosote bushes. A dike, a green belt, and lakes now control runoff but occasionally streets without storm sewers can flood and impede the traveler. Indian Bend Wash still has its wild moments.

Dust bowl

When the rainy season subsides, the sun bakes the silt of the valley. The drier it gets the less compacted it becomes. Many times we drove axle deep through ruts of dust. During this severe drought in the spring of 1937 we started our annual trek from winter camp at Taliesin West over desert roads to Scottsdale. Dust surged up to the hub caps and sifted into every crack of our station wagon. As we continued making our way to Wisconsin that spring, the impact of the drought became apparent. Driving through Texas, Oklahoma, Missouri, Arkansas, and Illinois, we encountered devastation everywhere.

The dust in our wooden station wagon forced us to wear wet cloths over our faces in order to breathe. Along the way dead, bloated cattle lined the fields. Drifts of dust swept over the roofs of abandoned houses and barns. No greenery appeared anywhere, just expanses of scorched earth.

Upon arrival we discovered our valley in Wisconsin also suffered. All the farmers were hurting. Some of our people, unable to sleep in the scorching night air, wrapped themselves in wet sheets and wandered over the parched grass of our Hill Garden trying to get relief. One of our sheet-clad girls fell over the stone wall and landed in a prickly juniper. We had to take her indoors and, with tweezers, pluck juniper out of her bottom.

Mr. Wright acquired a documentary film to show, called *The Plow that Broke the Plains*, in our theater. Mr. Wright invited all the local farmers to a Sunday afternoon showing. Financially, they all experienced desperate straits, with no crops, dry stubble fields, and emaciated or dying animals. In this stifling heat, they came into the theater to watch the government film, which emphasized the causes of the drought: the thoughtless logging of timber that had held moisture in the soil and the plowing of the plains with random furrows that incurred erosion.

In the film, rain pelted the muddy fields, making rivulets of the top soil that combined into dashing streams that carried the mud of our fertile soil to the sea. In the terrible heat of the theater, the atmosphere became tense. Suddenly, a great clap of thunder exploded over us! A cloudburst! Rain pounded the roof. With one accord, the farmers rose and filed out into the rain. They stood silently in the downpour with rain and tears streaking their faces. The deep feeling of this group of powerful men made such an impression on me that I can't speak of it to this day without choking with emotion.

Festivals

Festivals have always been beautiful occasions at both Taliesins. At Thanksgiving, Mr. Wright decorated U-shaped tables with garlands of fruit: pineapples, apples, oranges, tangerines, bananas, and grapefruit, with final touches of luscious clusters of grapes, nuts, and cranberries.

At my first Thanksgiving in Wisconsin, Mr. Wright asked us to tell what Thanksgiving meant to us. At a complete loss for something to say, and noticing that the snow had begun to fall outside, I sang Schubert's song:

When the snow flies in my face
Off I gayly brush it.
When my heart pains in my breast
Loud I sing to hush it.
Joyfully, we face the world
Facing wind and weather.
If there be no gods on earth
We'll be gods together.

Thanksgiving was not the only time Mr. Wright asked us to speak. He and Mrs. Wright devised a program for the chapel based somewhat on Ralph Waldo Emerson's essays. Each person had to be responsible for a Sunday program and a talk based on a quality that he or she most lacked—obedience, prudence, etc. For that day, the person had the responsibility not only for giving the talk but also for conducting the music and preparing and serving the lunch. I think this was just about our most difficult assignment and also the most unpopular. After the first round, we abandoned this project by common consent.

Training programs at Taliesin have always gone far beyond the normal disciplines, especially our Easter festival. For many years in Arizona we've spent our evenings and days before Easter painting goose eggs as favors for our guests. For elaborate designs it was not unusual to spend three or four hours painting an egg. Everyone participated, sitting around tables strewn with paint tubes, silently concentrating on his or her production.

As Easters came and went, the guest list grew out of proportion to our capacity, and we had to give up this tradition. To paint 250 eggs took too much time away from the heavy load of architectural work in the studio. But before we stopped this practice, our distinguished guests, bent on adding to their collections, started stealing eggs from one another's place. This caused so much friction that we had to wrap each egg in clear plastic with the name of the guest inside so that exchange was impossible. People of the area still compare their collections, indulging in one-upmanship. Now children have an egg dying party, making bright colored hens' eggs for all the tables.

The Easter brunch still consists of the traditional dishes of baba and pascha cheese introduced by Mrs. Wright. The preparations for making pascha cheese begin on Thursday. For 250 people, we have to stem twenty-four pounds of raisins. We enlist house guests, and a

Easter gathering at Taliesin West

congenial group gathers in the garden for stemming and visiting. Meanwhile, another group gathers to press seven pounds of blanched, ground almonds through fine sieves to make a light nut powder. These ingredients are set aside until Friday when they are combined with dry cottage cheese, butter, sugar, and vanilla, blended thoroughly, and packed into wooden truncated molds lined with cheese cloth, and stored in the cooler to drain.

Meanwhile, baba making is in process. On Friday at 6:30 A.M., twelve or fifteen people line up by the kitchen counter to separate about 500 eggs, as only the yolks are used. Butter, flour, yeast, and sugar are added to make a rich dough, which must be beaten or kneaded until large bubbles burst on the surface. After it has risen and been kneaded down

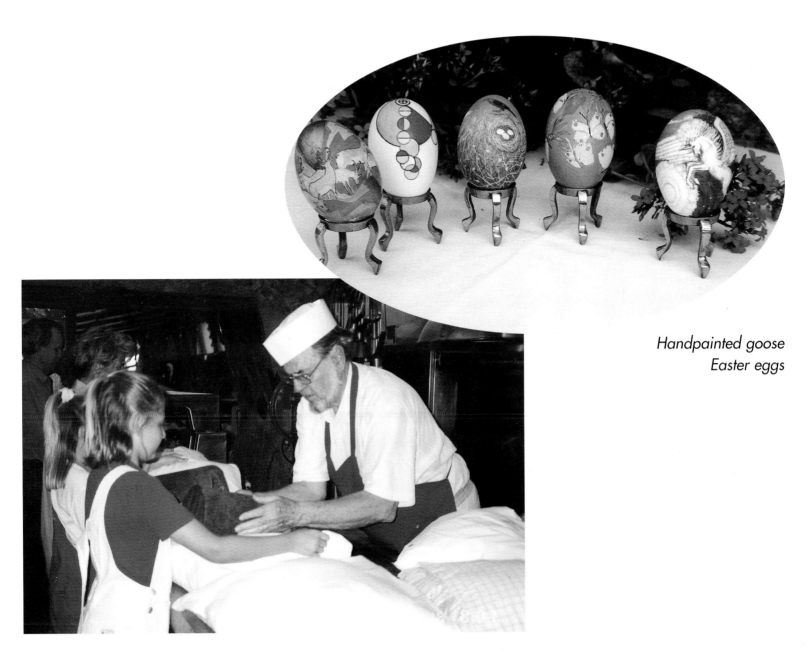

Handpainted goose
Easter eggs

Tom Casey showing the children how to roll the baba on a pillow

again, it is divided into tall cylindrical paper molds and set to rise again. After baking, the bread is extremely light and falls unless each loaf is carefully rolled on a pillow until cool. It is usually ready for rolling from two to four in the afternoon. Again, a group gathers with bed pillows covered with clean pillow slips and dish towels. The baba rolling begins. As each loaf cools, we strip away the paper and store the bread for Sunday's breakfast.

On Saturday morning, eggs are boiled, and Kay and John Rattenbury have a children's egg dying party in their garden. This usually ends up with some children as colorful as the sixty dozen eggs.

Meanwhile, round tables and chairs for 250 people are set up in readiness for

Table setting in the Cabaret Theatre for formal dinner with guests

decorating on Sunday either on the Sunset Terrace, in the pergola, in the garden squares near our pavilion, or most recently in our Apprentice Court. Tubs of spring flowers from the Japanese gardens are stored in a shady spot where, on

Sunday morning, the girls and house guests gather to make arrangements for each table.

Action begins at 6:30 Sunday morning. A group of young people, directed by Joe Fabris, blow up balloons with helium and weave them together with twine into strands, twenty or thirty feet long. As the balloons float from the buildings and gardens, they beckon guests coming from Scottsdale and Phoenix.

Tables, set with yellow cloths, flowers, strawberries, tall babas cut into horizontal slices, platters of pascha cheese, Easter eggs, and Easter candies greet the guests. The children race across the lawn, filling their Easter baskets as they search under bushes for hidden eggs. When everyone has gathered, we have a program of Easter music given by the chorus in the Pavilion.

At breakfast, old friends enjoy the traditional Taliesin feast and champion eggs emerge as people vie with one another in hand-to-hand egg combat. After breakfast, the long strands of balloons are gathered together. An Easter basket carrying eggs and a Taliesin card is securely tied to the floating bouquet and sent aloft. Many times the card has been returned—once from Arkansas, the farthest flight recorded.

When the balloons went south to Tucson we received a letter from a woman who had watched a man in an ultra-light plane intentionally fly into the balloons to break them. Instead, he tangled with the strings and crash landed. The incensed woman assured us we had no reason to stop sending our balloons abroad.

Another balloon flight ended in a dry wash in New Mexico where a group of children herded cattle. As the gift of balloons drifted down from the sky, the children were enthralled and delighted. They had their parents send an invitation for the whole Fellowship to visit their ranch.

Some messages have not been returned for many weeks, but considering the wide open spaces and woods of the West's remote areas, it is always astonishing that any of the balloons are found.

Strengthening the heartbeat

Music has always played an important part in Taliesin life. In the early years, Mr. Wright bought instruments for those who wanted to learn. Recorders became popular. Svetlana, an accomplished pianist and violinist, struggled to develop a string quartet with us amateurs. Mr. Wright affectionately dubbed it "The Farmer-Labor Quartet." We began to have formal evenings on Saturdays and Sundays, with dinner followed by a movie or music. We wear our best evening clothes at these

Cornelia in a cabaret scene from dance/drama performance by Iovanna

occasions. In his autobiography Mr. Wright called these evenings a chance for the Fellowship—"looking like the wrath of God during the week"—to wash behind the ears, put on raiment for the evening and try to find its measure in its manners, in other words, to develop the social graces.

From time to time we had guest artists perform for these evenings, such as the New York Quartet that played ancient instruments like the viola d'amore and viola da gamba; later, Anton Ravinsky, the pianist, came as did Carol Robinson. For several summers string quartets from the Chicago and Indianapolis symphonies visited us regularly, and their members gave lessons to our struggling musicians.

Mr. and Mrs. Wright's daughter, Iovanna Lloyd Wright, became accomplished on the harp, and her teacher, Marcel Grandjany, stayed at Taliesin for a summer. Tony Bek led one of our earliest musical groups, an *a cappella* chorus. With the swelling tide of the years, an ensemble, a string quartet, and other musical groups developed under the leadership of such fine musician-apprentices as Curtis Besinger, John Hill, John Amarantides, Bruce Brooks Pfeiffer, Vern Swaback, Susan Lockhart, and Effi Casey.

Flower arranging has always been a special activity at Taliesin. Mr. Wright spent many hours teaching us which branches could be arranged best to decorate the house or theater and which wild flowers made attractive bouquets. During Wisconsin winters we depended on evergreen branches—arbor vitae, pine, and juniper—and on bittersweet and antimony (wild field balsam or cudweed) for decoration. In the spring, we enjoyed blossoms of wild crab, hawthorn, wild plum, honeysuckle, and lilacs. Later came the flowers of the high-bush cranberries, which in the fall have brilliantly colored leaves and brilliant berries, as does the bittersweet of our woods. In Wisconsin, prairie flowers are everywhere: pasque flowers and trillium in the spring; lady slippers, butterfly weed, gentian, Queen Anne's lace, phlox, bouncing Bet, joe pye weed, swamp milkweed, ironweed, old field balsam, and many others throughout the season. All of these found their way into our flower arrangements.

During all this activity, working side by side with Mr. and Mrs. Wright, we apprentices also absorbed philosophy and architectural ideas. We learned to construct and maintain buildings, to decorate them, and to enjoy them. Work proceeded on the Hillside buildings. We remodeled the theater several times before it arrived at its present state.

When I first came to the Fellowship, rural electrification had not reached our area of Wisconsin. Mr. Wright had dammed the stream to supply power for a hydroelectric generator. Sometimes, in the midst of a formal musical evening, the lights would dim to a blackout, and someone would say, "Oh, oh! There's a turtle in the dynamo." An apprentice would run down the hill with a flashlight to extricate the offender while we waited to finish the concert. When electricity finally came to our area, Mr. Wright insisted that it be put underground throughout the valley. Not one electric nor telephone pole mars the vista in the valley.

We still enjoy the diverse social life of our two Taliesins. Their distinctive buildings, their courtyards, terraces, and grounds inspire many creative occasions, parties, and picnics. The heartbeat of Taliesin Fellowship—its music, architecture, and art, in harmony with nature—remains strong.

Creative parties

Throughout our life, creative parties have been a part of Taliesin. Mrs. Wright had a remarkable sense for putting together meaningful parties. Once she organized a "heaven and hell" party, with the idea that those who had contributed to the good of the world ascended to heaven and those with negative life force descended to hell. Everyone became an actor in an assigned part— Henry the Eighth to hell and Margaret

Heloise Crista, Iovanna Lloyd Wright, and Pat Percy dressed for a performance

Gary Herberger (center) in a performance of Mary Magdalene

Kenn Lockhart (center) in costume drama

Ling Po as a sherpa in a dramatic performance

"Spanish galleon"

Sanger and John the Baptist to heaven, etc. The men constructed a great set by the lake, with a high tower for heaven and a lowly area for hell.

They completed it at noon, after several days' labor. At four that afternoon a big storm blew in and leveled the whole set. By seven our determined men rebuilt it before the guests would arrive. The chorus came down the lake on a splendid galleon carrying Abe Lincoln to heaven, singing, "Let the heavenly light shine on me." But as they got across the lake from the party, the boat's motor died. Frantically, they tried to man the oars, while the boat drifted toward the dam and the falls. Bravely, the chorus continued to repeat, "Let the heaven light shine on me. Let the heaven light shine on me. Let the heaven. . . ."

As the galleon neared the falls, the chorus voices sounded strained and frightened. Just then a gust of wind helped float them to shore and to help Abe Lincoln on his way to heaven. Everyone came ashore, walking on water, that is, they walked on a plank concealed two inches under the surface. Someone accidentally slipped off the plank and fell into the lake. John the Baptist (Dick Carney dressed in sheepskins) emerged from the trees bellowing, "Oh, ye of little faith." Five-year old Susie Montooth, dressed like an angel, was supposed to climb to the top of the tower of heaven, stop a moment on a small platform, and descend to the other side to allow room for the next person. But Susie refused to leave. She said, "I'm an angel, I'm supposed to be in heaven, and I'm going to stay here!"

At one Arizona party for Clare Booth Luce, we all represented masterpieces of famous sculptors, such as Henry Moore's *Statue of a Woman* and Michaelangelo's *David*. Concealed by white tights, leotards, and caps, with faces and hands whitened, Michael Sutton represented David, and I had to lie on the stage in the position of Moore's woman.

In one skit, Dick Carney assumed the role of Icarus, a figure from mythology. He was supposed to fly across the living room harnessed to a rope, but things went awry, and he hung swinging in the air. At every tug of the rope he swung back and forth banging his head on the balcony.

Skits have always been popular. Sometimes we have wig parties, where everyone tries to change his or her image by a hair creation. Many parties have beautiful and elaborate sets, such as the one given on our island in Wisconsin as a benefit for the American Players Theatre. Large clusters of balloons, interspersed with twinkling Italian lights, floated above the party and arched high above the stage. Torches encircled the stage and flared from the lake. Lighted candles drifted over the water, while fireworks burst in the sky. Our chorus sang German *lieder* and spirituals; Heloise Crista's dance group performed exercises in coordination; and the apprentices did a humorous take-off on Shakespeare's *The Tempest*. All the fairies (men six feet and over, wearing skimpy tutus) plunged into the lake to rescue the shipwrecked travelers.

After some of us returned from a trip to South Africa where Mrs. Wright gave a lecture in Durban, we had a skit party about coming through customs. Bruce Brooks Pfeiffer performed one of the final acts. With his entourage of Ubangi wives he declared ten of his wives as property. The customs man asked, "What about this little one, the eleventh one?" "Oh," said Bruce, "she doesn't count. She's lunch." "Lunch" happened to be Sarah Logue who, furious with Bruce, may never have forgiven him.

At one time, in order to entertain some of our older guests, Mrs. Wright gave a waltz party. We girls wore formal ball gowns and white gloves, black tie for the men. Everyone practiced waltzes, polkas, and schottisches to lead the guests. Our elderly friends, many of whom hadn't danced for a long time, enjoyed the old familiar steps.

Some skits became all-time favorites, requested at every party. Michael Sutton did one such skit pantomiming the time he served Mr. and Mrs. Wright. While carrying a platter of steak, he had to step over Casanova, Mrs. Wright's weimaraner. As he did so, the dog reared up between his legs. When the steak flew

Cornelia and Leslie Lockhart (Bisharat) in Time Upon Time *dance/drama*

Cornelia and Tom Casey as Mae West and W. C. Fields

into the air, Michael tried to grab it, but Casanova snapped it up and made off with it. Michael was a real ham and did friendly imitations of all of us.

Tom Casey and I could ham it up too in a popular skit of W. C. Fields and Mae West. We changed our lines according to our audience. For instance, in entertaining a group of visiting public relations men, Mae said "I've never been interested in public relations!" It brought down the house. With a large bulbous nose applied, Tom not only looked like W. C. Fields but was a master at imitating him.

The skits went on and on, sometimes exploring the realm of ancient myth or the work and lives of famous architects or other notables. Over the years, many people at Taliesin became fine actors and imitators. Iovanna, Mr. and Mrs. Wright's daughter, always gave a superb performance as did Kay and John Rattenbury, William Wesley Peters, Heloise Crista, my daughter Indira, and many others. Skits still enliven and enlighten the life at Taliesin.

Weekends

Weekend activities have a special place at Taliesin, requiring extra effort on all fronts. In Wisconsin Mr. Wright would sometimes invite ten or fifteen overnight

Dick Carney and Kay Rattenbury at a skit party

guests for our Saturday and Sunday activities, often to Mrs. Wright's dismay as she knew the amount of work involved. In the early years each person became responsible for many jobs because of our limited number of apprentices.

Cornelia performs as an evangelist

Preparing for houseguests

Those in the kitchen busily churned butter, made cottage cheese, baked bread and pastries, and prepared quantities of garden vegetables. Picking enough peas or beans for fifteen extra guests took a lot of time; preparing them meant tedious work. A lucky kitchen helper could get the people at four o'clock tea to help shell peas or snap beans.

The cook had to catch fifteen or twenty hens in the chicken coop, chop off their heads, and defeather them after loosening the feathers by plunging the hens into boiling water. The innards were removed and the chickens made ready for roasting in our big black wood-burning stove. Almost everything served—chickens, pork, beef, vegetables, and fruit—we grew organically and raised on our farm.

Besides additional cooking, we had to make up guest rooms with sheets, pillowcases, towels, and spreads, all of which meant extra laundry for Monday morning. Having no such thing as automatic dryers, loads of sheets, towels, tablecloths, and several hundred napkins had to be hung out in the yard, and they sometimes froze stiff in icy weather. Such was the prelude to ironing.

Guest rooms, dining rooms, the living room and loggia of the house, the studio, and Hillside Theatre needed thorough cleaning, after which we decorated with many varieties of wild flowers and branches.

Unexpected help

Once it happened to be my turn to make up rooms for fifteen guests and also to clean the theater. By starting early in the morning I managed to finish the guest rooms by mid-afternoon. Just as I prepared to walk over the hill to tackle the theater, Mrs. Wright called me to her room. She immediately saw I was exhausted and asked, "Where are you going?"

"To decorate the theater."

"That's a big job," she said. "Did you ask someone to help?"

"Yes, several people, but I couldn't persuade them to join me."

"Well, I won't keep you," she said.

I went on my way and had just started gathering supplies in the theater when both Mr. and Mrs. Wright appeared to help. Together we swept the floor, dusted the chairs, gathered wood for the fireplace, and filled the flower containers with water. Out on the grounds we cut honeysuckle, oak, and pine branches to make arrangements for the theater.

Humming as he adjusted a branch, Mr. Wright was thoroughly enjoying himself. Arranging foliage was one of his greatest pleasures. I think it took him back to his youth when he decorated the family chapel. After we finished our work, he sat at the piano and improvised with rich quiet chords. With all this loving help and enthusiasm from Mr. and Mrs. Wright, my exhaustion vanished. I even felt rejuvenated for the evening's entertainment.

Formal and informal dining

At that time, we had formal dinners on both Saturday and Sunday evenings. Saturday dinners, served in the theater, were followed by a movie. On Sunday afternoon the public saw the same movie for an admission fee of fifty cents that included homemade cookies and coffee served in a gold embossed red lacquer demitasse. These elegant little handleless cups soon vanished as people slipped them into their pockets as souvenirs.

Before the Sunday afternoon theater, we gathered for late morning picnics. These included treks into distant hills, either with horses and carriages or by cars. Once settled by a stream or river or

A picnic at "Little Norway," Wisconsin.
John Lautner (standing) and Gene Masselink (kneeling)
with Mr. Wright in the background.

65

Mr. Wright supervising the grill at a picnic

on a cliff overlooking the valleys, we built fires to roast hot dogs or hamburgers, bake potatoes and ears of corn in the ashes, and heat the homemade buns. After a feast with the usual picnic garnishes of Wisconsin cheese, apple sauce, cottage cheese, and pickles, we topped off the meal with Taliesin spice cake or apple pie made with apples from our orchard.

Some high sandstone cliffs exposed by waters from the glaciers became our favorite picnic spots. Pines crest the cliffs; huckleberries grow among the boulders; ferns, Solomon Seal, red-berried Mountain Ash, and other foliage of the lush forests grew on steep hillsides. Lichen and moss-covered boulders made favorite seats among the pine needles at our feet. We enjoyed the spectacular distant views of the valleys below as we ate our picnic meal.

Borglum Rock became the scene of one of Mr. Wright's best known photographs. At that time Gutzon Borglum was sculpting the presidents' heads on Mount Rushmore. He and Mr. Wright had great rapport. Mr. Wright introduced me to him saying, "Meet Cornelia. She is a fine piece of architecture." Mr. Borglum seemingly agreed and said he would like to do a sculpture of me. His visit was brief, and he died shortly after, so this piece of architecture missed being captured in stone!

Even though we picnicked Sunday morning and had theater in the afternoon, the evening continued with a formal dinner in the Taliesin living room. We served on small individual tables set with napkins and silverware. Dinner in this remarkably beautiful and fine acoustical space was followed by chorus, string quartet, and piano music. Occasionally guest artists added to our entertainment.

The men wore black ties and tuxedos and the girls evening dresses. Whenever Mr. and Mrs. Wright arrived, their regal presence always added a special elegance. Though she had little money during those Depression years, Mrs. Wright managed to find ways to help the young apprentices improve their appearances. Sometimes she outfitted the women by sacrificing one of her few dresses or just helped them change a hairdo or makeup. Often she persuaded someone more affluent to help dress a person who needed a lift. We all exchanged or loaned evening dresses or other clothes just as do brothers and sisters. Now at Taliesin we continue to share. Actually, because of our common goals and long years of working together, we are closer to one another than most family members.

We still have remarkable weekend entertainment at our formal Saturday evening gatherings. In deference to changing lifestyles, some of our activities have changed, but the spirit of creating beautiful occasions remains a Fellowship priority.

THOSE WHO PASSED BY

The Lloyd Jones

Over the years, Mr. Wright's mother's clan, the Lloyd Jones', became part of our extended family. The Andrew Porters (Mr. Wright's sister Jane, her husband Andrew, and son Franklin,) lived across the hill at Tan-y-deri. Mr. Wright's sister, Maginel Barney; her daughter Bitsy (the writer Elizabeth Enright Gillham); Bitsy's son Nicky; and his nanny came from New York to spend the summers. Mr. Wright's children and their families visited periodically, and at one time or another, several grandchildren—Catherine Baxter's daughter Ann, John's daughter Elizabeth, Lloyd's son Eric, Lewellyn's sons Thomas and Timothy (Tommy and Timmy) and Frances Suppes' daughter Nora—all spent summers or joined the Fellowship for extended periods.

For reunions at the chapel in the valley, hundreds of Lloyd Jones' descendants of Mr. Wright's mother and uncles trickle in from all over the continent. The Lloyd Jones Chapel, (designed by Silsbee in 1886) is our meeting place for weddings, concerts, lectures, funerals, and reunions.

When I first arrived, cousin Mary Lloyd Jones from Tulsa came for the summer. Some family members and many locals were convinced the Fellowship couldn't survive the Depression. Not so, cousin Mary. She had great faith in Mr. and Mrs. Wright and the Fellowship. As she came to the Sunday afternoon movies with fifty cents admission in hand she often delightedly announced that Bisser (Florence Lloyd Jones), her favorite niece and teenage second cousin of Mr. Wright, was coming from Tulsa. We all looked forward to her visits. Bisser has two brothers, Jenkin and Richard, who at that time were carefree college boys enrolled at the University of Wisconsin in Madison. They visited Mr. and Mrs. Wright on weekends but never had much to do with us apprentices. Years later all three children inherited their father's newspaper, *The Tulsa Tribune*, and Jenkin became editor and publisher. In 1992 he wrote this letter to Richard Carney, our CEO. It explains much about how he and many other people viewed the Fellowship in those early lean years:

November 30, 1992

Dear Mr. Carney:

Tennyson once wrote of "Old forgotten far-off things and battles long ago." The cold embers of old recollections blazed again when I read the fall 1992 issue of the Frank Lloyd Wright Quarterly *and particularly the article by Cornelia Brierly.*

One might say that I antedate Cornelia. She arrived in 1934. I was a senior at the University of Wisconsin, Madison, in the fall of '32 when Wright started his school. But, as Frank's second cousin, I was a frequent moocher at Sunday night suppers at Taliesin from the fall of '29 until my graduation.

When I understood what Wright proposed, I was sure it couldn't last. Slave labor has been outlawed in the United States since 1863 and here was slave labor with refinements undreamed of by Simon Legree. Not only were the young laborers paid nothing for growing food crops and restoring buildings in advanced states of decay but they were charged for the privilege. I shamefully underestimated the magic of Frank and Olgivanna. I watched the peasants labor in a drafting room made of green lumber because Frank couldn't afford kiln-dried. I saw them eagerly consume concentration camp cuisine. In spite of gross exploitation they gathered worshipfully around their two gurus, male and female, and the talk was not only stratospheric but often incomprehensible to me. Here was Plato. Here was Joan of Arc. No matter that Frank was far overdue on payments for his front-wheel-drive Cord automobile. No matter that the Sunday supplement scribblers were still nipping at his heels. There was a spurious opulence in the midst of near starvation. Bittersweet and pussy willows, gathered in the bog across the road, adorned the living room. Apples from the orchard overflowed the bowls.

Oscar Wilde once sniffed a rose and said, "I have had my dinner." A pragmatic Oklahoma college kid was amazed at the power of style. Wes Peters, an Indiana editor's son, was one of the first disciples. He never left. There may have been nothing on the table but soup and dark brown bread, but Olgivanna would trot out a jar of Montenegrin plum jam, which she called pavidla, and we all feasted.

It was my personal privilege to see Frank Lloyd Wright at the nadir of his fortunes and live to die at the height of his fame and fortune. It was no tribute to my intelligence, back in 1932, that, when I watched a handful of my contemporaries hammering, sawing, whitewashing under conditions of a Spartan camp, I couldn't imagine what held them together.

Very truly yours,

Jenkin Lloyd Jones

Marya Lilien

As a student at the Carnegie Institute of Technology (now Carnegie Mellon) I went yearly to study the International Art Exhibit at Carnegie Museum. A striking portrait of an elegant lady in blue gloves, painted by Antoni Mickalak, fascinated me. Her image remained fixed in my mind.

Marya Lilien

After my first year at Taliesin, a Polish lady named Marya Lilien came to visit. There before me stood the lady of the portrait! Mr. and Mrs. Wright invited her to join the Fellowship for a year. Marya, already a practicing architect in Poland, had many talents. Using her old world recipes she contributed delicious treats—such as the flourless nut cake embellished with strawberry jam and whipped cream and smothered with chocolate—a delicacy from the peasants of the Tatra Mountains.

On formal evenings she entertained us with Polish folk songs and German lieder. Sometimes while we sat in the Tea Circle shelling peas or stringing beans, Marya told stories of her childhood in Poland—how she and her cousins picked wild strawberries in the mountains or how, during rose season, they helped their mother prepare the petals for jelly. All the children sat in the garden around a pile of rose petals. With small scissors they snipped the bitter yellow end off each petal while they sang folk songs.

Marya became such an integral member of our Fellowship family that we missed her when she had to return to Poland in 1937. She lived in an apartment in Lvov when World War II broke out. The bombing sent all the tenants to the basement. Marya was desperately trying to find a way to leave Poland. One day after weeks of confinement, she ran upstairs to look for something in the vacant apartment. The telephone rang. A voice said, "If you come immediately we have a car going to the border." Packing two handbags she rushed to join her friends.

Along the way when they had to abandon the car because of incessant bombing, they crawled through ditches and rode on a farmer's hay wagon. When they reached a village on the Romanian border, the farmer directed Marya to a peasant's home where she asked a young woman for a room. An old grandfather entered. He said, "The Polish Army is marching out and the Russian Army is coming across the border. If you want to escape you'd better go right away." Marya left immediately and begged a Polish officer to hide her in his vehicle as they crossed the border to Romania. They left her on a street corner. A stranger from the underground approached her. "If you drop your bags and follow me I can help you." This she did, and after much delay managed to get back to the United States.

Our democratic government fascinated Marya. When she heard about Herbert Hoover staying at the hotel in

Chandler, she rushed to see him. To Marya, he had become the hero who fed Europe after the First World War.

When at election time we all went to the local poll to vote in Wisconsin, Marya, who had just come to America, asked if she could go to watch. At the poll the people said, "Here comes Wright's crowd," and without question handed us all ballots. When we got home Marya, in a high state of excitement went to Hans Koch, our master crafts-man, who was not a citizen but had been in this country many years. He and Marya had spent hours discussing the election. "Hans," Marya said, "you must go to the poll to vote. They gave me a ballot and I voted for Roosevelt." In due time Marya did become a citizen, and for many years she taught at the Art Institute in Chicago where she founded the Department of Design. Her success-ful students work in many areas of design throughout the country and have established "The Marya Lilien Foundation."

Marya remained a loyal friend to Taliesin ever since her first visit in 1936. By some miraculous circumstance her beautiful portrait from Poland was returned to her. Recently Marya retired to her homeland and left the famous portrait in the care of a nephew.

Original gymnasium stage

Paul Robeson and theater renovation

When Mr. Wright's Aunt Jane and Aunt Nell operated the Hillside Home School, a building Mr. Wright had designed for them, the room that became our theater served as a rectangular gymnasium. It had a very small stage at one side and a surrounding balcony used by the stu-dents for races, official or otherwise.

Over the years Mr. Wright modified this space to exemplify a very different grammar.

By 1934, when I arrived, he had added wooden benches with cushions. Broad horizontal boards attached to the backs of the benches served as tables for the seats directly behind, and our formal Saturday night dinners took place there. Following dinner, we had our own musi-cal programs and the best of foreign films.

Paul Robeson outside the Hillside Theater

Left to right: (front row) Carry Caraway, friend of Robeson, Paul Robeson Jim Thomson, Mrs. Wright, Betty Barnsdall
(second row) Cornelia, Burt Goodrich, Noverre Musson, Earl Friar, Karl Monrad, Edgar Tafel, John Lautner, Benny Dombar, Jack Howe, Everett Baker, Gene Masselink

Once, while Mr. Wright was away lecturing, Paul Robeson, the well-known singer and actor, came to visit and offered to give a program in the theater. His great size and magnificent spirit filled the small stage as he spoke, sang, and demonstrated the origin of spirituals. He said that when visiting Africa he found his own heritage close to that of the tribes. He could leap into the moving circle of dancers and follow every rhythm.

Robeson's father, a Southern minister, originated spirituals in his church every Sunday. After the sermon, he would step down from the pulpit to join the congregation. Bending low and singing in a rich, deep voice, he would start a rhythm, "Brother, give me your hand! Brother, give me your hand!" Soon, the whole congregation, with joined hands, moved in a circle chanting, "Brother, give me your hand!" With variations on the original theme, each Sunday they created a new spiritual.

Mr. Robeson said African languages rested upon a tonal quality that made possible the relay of messages over long distances by the tonal sounds of the drum beat. Understanding these tonal sounds made it easy for him to learn Chinese and Russian, which, he said, depend largely on similar tonal qualities.

Mr. Robeson had so stimulated us that when Mr. Wright returned he heard many glowing accounts of the performance. To our astonishment, it upset Mr. Wright that Mrs. Wright had invited a African American man to perform at Taliesin. Then we realized what a terrible scar had been left from the early Taliesin tragedy when a African American man went berserk and axed down the people Mr. Wright loved. With Mrs. Wright's patient help, this wound finally healed so that, eventually, he welcomed black students and friends.

It may have been because of Robeson's visit—because afterwards we all commented on the smallness of the stage—that Mr. Wright determined to reconstruct the theater. At that time, we showed foreign films to the public on Sunday afternoons. For fifty cents they saw the best movies of the times and enjoyed coffee and cookies by the fire. Therefore, any remodeling of the theater had to be accomplished during the week. With his cane as baton, Mr. Wright directed the boys, who wielded wrecking bars and shovels, to tear out existing partitions and floors, lower the stage, and angle new partitions so as to change the rectilinear box-like room into an area of flowing planes and extended space.

These "pushes" for remodeling extended over a period of years and usually involved many all-day, all-night sessions. Mr. Wright always directed the projects, taking ten-minute catnaps, and then remaining awake throughout the rest of the procedure. While the men rebuilt, the girls made new cushions and curtains and served midnight lunches of sandwiches and milk.

The final renovation of the theater occurred because of an accident in 1952. Mr. Wright wanted to burn brush by the building. When the fire wouldn't catch well he sent Davy Davison to Taliesin for more matches, but before Davy returned, the wind changed. Suddenly, the fire swept out of control, igniting the dry timbers of the theater. Every part except the masonry burned, as did the dining area and the classrooms above it. Neighbors gathered from everywhere. Mr. Wright tried to enter the flaming building to retrieve art objects, but the "Lady Logger," a powerful woman from Spring Green grabbed him around the chest and said, "Frank, you can't do that!" She saved his life. The fire stopped just as it reached and charred the first beams of the Hillside living room. Consequently, that great historic room where Mr. Wright "broke the box" remains intact to this day.

With all his super energy, Mr. Wright rebuilt the theater, lowering the floor once more to expand the space. He covered some wall corners with mitered mirrors to continue the obliteration of the box. He mounted new chairs of the design made for the Guggenheim Museum's theater on angles to the stage The men upholstered the chairs with comfortable, rose velour cushions. Mr. Wright designed unusual hanging light fixtures constructed of the same wood as the theater. The balcony disappeared in favor of cantilevered wooden acoustical panels.

The balcony had become a hazard because of the trespassing public. Once during a movie, in the darkened theater some college boys pushed their way onto the balcony from the upper hall. As they noisily pushed and shoved, they catapulted one of their crowd over the balcony. He landed below, grazing Mr. Wright, and thereby breaking his fall. As the fellow hastily picked himself up, Mr. Wright, stunned by the unexpected blow, furiously berated him for trespassing. The boy, with the rest of his gang, rushed out of the theater never to be seen again.

Since the fire had wiped out the decorative items, including a rug that I had designed and hooked, Mr. Wright created many new features. Greatest among them was the richly conceived abstract curtain design of the Wisconsin hills, clouds, birds, and trees. As a birthday surprise for Mr. Wright, the apprentices appliquéd brightly colored felt on Peruvian linen to complete the resplendent design.

The theater has long ceased to be open to the public for movies, though it has continued to be open for tours and special occasions. But the Fellowship members have, for many years, enjoyed musical evenings and movies there with our guests.

Maginel and Bitsy

Summers in Wisconsin developed into busy, fascinating times, with many interesting guests. Mr. Wright's sister, Maginel Wright Barney, spent her summers with us. Maginel, full of fun and very sophisticated, always enjoyed doing some summer project. Mrs. Wright taught us all to embroider felt with yarn to make colorful vests and jackets. These inspired Maginel to design yarn "paintings," which she sold in New York the next fall.

Sitting on the screened porch at Tan-y-deri, Maginel surrounded herself with colorful yarns that she used to recreate the scenes of the valley beyond the fields of grain and the pastures. She usually tucked a typical Wisconsin red barn into the picture. Mr. Wright's daughter, Frances, ran America House in New York and sold Maginel's creations, including many embroidered slippers.

Maginel's daughter, Bitsy Gillham (Elizabeth Enright, the author of short stories and children's books) and I were great friends. Bitsy had an old herb book, and we spent time thumbing through it and roaming through the meadows looking for herbs to make secret potions. One was a complexion concoction made of elderberry blossoms that, in aging, became more and more odoriferous, until we, by necessity, abandoned the whole gallon of stench. We tried making fruit brandies with pure alcohol, as well as other equally potent drinks. But most of all we enjoyed the companionship.

Bitsy, a very creative and beautiful girl, had married Bob, an advertising manager for Paramount Studios, who could never spend much time with us in the summer. But Bitsy told me stories of the Hollywood stars she'd met, many of whom became her friends. She always came to Taliesin with her young son, Nicky, and his nurse, Nana. She based many of her children's stories on her summers with us at Taliesin, especially

Bitsy Gillham and son Nicky

Thimble Summer, one of her most successful books. For her writing, Bitsy used her maiden name.

With Bitsy and others at Taliesin, I took in the country wedding dances that featured local bands in barn-like structures with names like Rainbow Gardens or Lilac Gardens. Sometimes we went to square dances, where the local experts usually became exasperated at our incompetence. We confused the squares. The calls of "allemande left" and "allemande right" could spell our Waterloo. The usual fee of a dime for entrance to the dance hall assured one of an indelible stamp on the wrist that could persist even after soap and water.

Our arriving home late from these dances upset Mr. Wright. Very often, after flattering ourselves in thinking that we got to our rooms without being heard, we would be called to account by Mr. Wright, with a lecture about profitless "boy and girl good times."

One summer evening at Taliesin as everything hummed with life and activity, we had a birthday party for Bitsy in the hill dining room. Mr. and Mrs. Wright had gone on a trip and intended to return the next day. When at home with us, their discipline and work gave a certain tension to our lives. Whenever they left for a few days, the cry would go up, "O.K. everybody, the lid's off!" Not that we did anything unseemly in their absence, but the atmosphere became more relaxed.

After Bitsy blew out the birthday candles, we all decided to go to a movie in Spring Green. Getting into the cars in the gravel courtyard, we discovered one car was out of gas. Our newest and youngest apprentice, Ellis Jacobs, had just joined the Fellowship. Taking advantage of our seniority, we said, "Ellis, get us some gas."

Obligingly, he opened the garage door where we kept a large tank of gas. In the dark Ellis didn't notice the pool of gas that had leaked from the tank. In order to see the gas cock, he lit a match. A horrendous explosion shook our cars. The blast blew Ellis thirty feet across the courtyard to the stone wall. Red faced, with singed eyebrows and hair, he stood by the wall in shock.

The giant oak tree by the garage burst with a roar of flames into a torch that beckoned farmers from miles around. Edgar Tafel leaped into a truck and drove it away from the conflagration. Soon the courtyard teamed with neighbors and firemen from Spring Green. While the firemen tried to get a hose down the hill to the lake, we formed a bucket brigade with every type of container we could

Bitsy and Nicky making wine

find. John Lautner went to the milk room where a trough of water held two five gallon cans of milk. Carrying a can in either hand, John dumped the milk into the fire truck, then went back to refill the cans with water.

The dry cedar shingles of the roof burned like kindling. To stop the fire from spreading, Edgar Tafel and Bob Mosher started axing the roof over the outdoor steps that separated the ice house from the main building. With the help of our people, neighbors, and firemen, we extinguished the fire that left a wet charred mess of shingles over the five horse stalls next to the garage.

We all knew we had to rebuild the roof before Mr. Wright returned. During the night and the next morning we continued the birthday party by reshingling. By late afternoon Mr. and Mrs. Wright arrived to see a completely new roof. Stunned when they learned the story of the fire, Mr. Wright's resigned comment (one that he often repeated) was: "Well boys, something always happens in the country." None of us ever forgot that birthday party.

TALES OF MY OWN

During the late thirties young families began to develop at Taliesin. My sister Hulda and Blaine Drake were married in the Taliesin living room with the blessing of Mr. and Mrs. Wright. Kay Schneider and Davy Davison and Polly (now Frances) and Kenn Lockhart married in the Lloyd Jones family chapel in our valley. Soon all had lively families of young boys and girls.

In the spring of 1938 Peter Berndtson, a blond, handsome, talented man of Swedish descent arrived at Taliesin. Both his mother and father had come to America from Sweden and settled in Methuen, Massachusetts, a suburb of Boston. Peter attended Massachusetts Institute of Technology until the Depression when his brother's bad investments depleted the substantial inheritance from his father. When he left for New York, he changed his name from Albert to Peter.

Peter survived the Depression in New York City by painting pictures that he exchanged in the Village for a bowl of soup and later by designing theater sets for summer stock. There he met and married Ruth Barstow, a vivacious, aspiring actress. Ruth came to Taliesin with him. Their marriage ended shortly thereafter, however, since Ruth missed the stage and decided to return to New York.

Peter separated from Ruth with many qualms. It was a hard choice, but he had set his heart on an architectural career. As an already accomplished architect, Mr. Wright encouraged him to pursue life at Taliesin. Peter traveled with the Fellowship to Taliesin West where

Peter Berndtson, 1945

building continued on our winter camp. In the spring of 1939 I became interested in Peter as he began to court me with parties in our tents and walks in the desert. We fell in love and married in a quiet ceremony. Eventually we had two girls, Anna and Indira, who became playmates with Brandoch Peters, Tal Davison, Peter and Eric Drake, and Brian and Leslie Lockhart, other children who grew up at Taliesin.

Mexican honeymoon

Throughout the years the Fellowship has enjoyed visits to our Mexican neighbors. When Peter and I decided to marry, Mr. and Mrs. Wright and our friends encouraged us to honeymoon in Mexico. Kay Schneider (later Kay Rattenbury) said, "I'll lend you my little red Bantam roadster."

"Great," we said. "We'll drive down the west coast to Mexico City."

Old timers warned that roads were impassable. Full of enthusiasm and confident that we could cope we said, "We'll go the native way. No Southern Pacific luxury hotels, just native inns and native restaurants." When we crossed the border at Nogales, we had no idea we would witness some of the dangers of the historic Peon Revolution of 1939.

After going a short distance from the border, we stopped for lunch at a low wooden building. Entering the building from the strong sunlight of outdoors, we blinked to adjust to the dark interior. Truck drivers seated on wooden benches lined along plank tables looked like rough characters, but they treated us as their guests, moving aside to make room.

In one corner of the room ample women in long black dresses and black mantillas cooked over a fire laid on the floor. Soon they distributed bowls of meat, beans, and tortillas to be passed around the table. Sampling the delicious food we felt we'd put the first "notch in our belts" for a real Mexican experience. Later, we gave that notch a second thought.

Setting forth, we hoped to make Hermosillo by nightfall. The sun was intense, but we couldn't put the top up as the car was loaded with baggage. Ruts got increasingly worse, with detours back and forth to a new roadbed. We shuttled up and down banks and washes that crossed and recrossed our path. Late in the evening, we arrived in Hermosillo where our small red car made an immediate hit with all the children. These little people clung to the car delightedly chanting, "Muy chiquito, muy chiquito" (very small, very cute) and "Radio!

Radio!" The car was so low that even the little children could lean over the doors as they examined the radio. With a slow, admiring procession of children clinging to the car, we drove through the town. An opera company from Mexico City played at the theater, and all the children begged to see the show. We bought tickets for some twenty or thirty children, but as soon as we got into the theater they dispersed like seeds bursting from a pod.

That night we parked outside the Hotel Roma next to one of the first small Willys cars. The next morning, the hotel clerk said, "My Willys she so proud. She think she have a child."

Then we were off to Guaymas, over the same rutted dirt roads and detours. Along the way we saw abandoned road builders' camps of open shelters made with thatched palm roofs. At one such place an enormous Indian woman loomed up from behind a bush gesturing and insisting on having a ride. A two-seater Bantam is no place to squeeze in a third passenger but, seeing her in this God-forsaken place, we hadn't the heart to abandon her. I moved as close to Peter as I could while she plumped into my seat, settling there like an overstuffed, sweaty, black sack, squeezing me into the crack between her mountainous form

Mexican honeymoon, 1939

and Peter. Before she got into the car, she produced two large bundles tied in black cloth, which we fastened onto the other luggage.

Groaning under the load, the little car could no longer make the grades. As it went up a bank, the car settled back on its haunches, dug into the sand and refused to move. Without a load the Bantam could easily be taken by the front bumper to turn it around, but with such a load it wouldn't budge. We tried to get the Indian woman to get out and help, but she was immobile, until she realized that one of her bundles had flown off into the dust, scattering its contents. With threatening gestures, she insisted all the pieces be retrieved. The contents included bits of tin foil, small pieces of dried orange peel, broken nails, and other debris left by the road gang. The woman couldn't bear to leave these valuable possessions.

Since we hadn't seen any houses or people for miles, we tried to learn her destination. "Rancho, rancho," she said, pointing ahead. In the blazing sun, we burned and sweltered and were beginning to feel the queasy effects of our native lunch from the day before.

After more road problems and detours, we finally spotted a ranch in the distance. "Great, let's take her to the ranch," Peter said. She objected violently. Nevertheless, we opened the gate and started driving toward the men in the distance who worked at a watering trough. They apparently recognized our passenger and began flailing hoes and shovels, shouting curses, and threatening us. Quickly we untied her bags. Furious and shrieking, she gathered her bundles as we hastily drove off.

We'd driven for about an hour when we discovered missing baggage. In our haste to get rid of the passenger, we'd loosened the ties. Bumping back over our tracks, we found the luggage just outside the ranch gate. It was evening when we drove into Guaymas—sunburned, covered with dust, sick with diarrhea, and exhausted. Driving down main street, an American in a big limousine drove alongside us and called, "My God, where'd you kids come from in that toy car?"

"Nogales," we said.

He looked incredulous and said, "Better come to my hotel and get cleaned up."

"No," we thanked him. "We're planning to go to a Mexican hotel."

"Those places are full of cockroaches and malarial mosquitoes."

Nonetheless, we picked a Mexican hotel. Accompanied by a loud, electric organ on the waterfront, plagued by mosquitoes, and weakened by constant trips to the bathroom, we suffered through the night. Every time the toilet flushed, water overflowed from the bathroom into our room. The shower leaked into a metal pan with a constant loud pling, pling, pling.

After this sleepless night, we welcomed the morning and went downstairs to breakfast where we found a long, dreary room and tables dressed with soiled, gray-tinged tablecloths. By the shuffle and pallor of our mumbling waiter, we decided he must have spent time in solitary confinement. So far, our "native experiences" didn't exactly match what we'd romanticized.

We inquired about the way south of Guaymas, only to be told cars could not drive over the impassable roads. The Yaqui Indians had just gone on a rampage and killed a group of engineers driving by in a station wagon. Recognizing defeat, we bargained to send the Bantam back to the border and continue by train. After much gesturing and bargaining in broken Spanish and broken English, we convinced the rail clerk that we wouldn't pay for an entire freight car to carry one Bantam roadster to the border. We finally compromised on a price.

This settled, we carried our bags to the nearest waterfront hotel. Entering the open patio, we were met by a barefoot boy. We tried to make him understand that we wanted a room for a few hours until the train came. Looking very knowing, he said the cost would be sixty-five cents and led us upstairs to a room overlooking the bay. We decided to take turns sleeping so that we wouldn't miss the train.

Since the door to the next room didn't quite shut, we could hear men playing cards there. Peter fell asleep and I was sitting on the bed half undressed when one of the burly men strolled into our room, eyed me casually, and walked out to our balcony. I wakened Peter. "Please, let's get out of here!" We dragged our baggage to the station, piled it on the tile benches and slept there until the midnight train arrived to shuttle us to the main line.

Getting on the air-conditioned Southern Pacific train was a real blessing. Mexico was in the throes of a labor revolution. There was much tension on the train. It was occasionally stopped by boulders placed on the track by white-clad peons who then faded into the night. Somehow without any accidents we settled down for an enjoyable trip. As we pulled into stations, Indians in native dress came to offer their wares of brightly colored serapes, fiber baskets, papayas, candied sweet potatoes, and hot food from their trainside braziers.

After arriving in Mexico City, we took trips to see the ancient pyramids, the floating gardens, and market places brilliant with flowers and tropical fruit. Everywhere people discussed labor unrest, with much talk of the train from Vera Cruz that had been blown up.

A group of Mexican artists were becoming internationally famous by their portrayal of the peons' problems. It was our good luck to be received by Diego Rivera, who, like a large friendly bear, padded around the room laying out his sketches and paintings on the floor before us. He was at the height of his productivity, championing the cause of the people. When we arrived in Guadalajara, we visited José Clemente Orozco, who also espoused the people's programs. We found this one-armed, powerful man on a high scaffold painting the ceiling of the orphanage.

In Guadalajara, the balcony of our hotel room overlooked the market place. We were serenaded by a Mariachi band while we watched the Indians in their traditional dress gathering from all the provinces, making a kaleidoscope of brilliant color as they moved about the market with crates of chickens, iguanas, baskets, and other wares. At our hotel, a handsome Indian stood at the door of the dining room spreading a pure white pelican pelt with a six-foot wingspread across his massive frame. He kept urging us to buy, but we didn't really know what to do with a pelican pelt. Finally, we succumbed to his charm and bought it for twelve pesos—$2.50 at that time.

The train returning to the border had a highly charged atmosphere. A notorious labor leader was aboard with his gunmen. He sat at a dining table with four gunmen facing him from opposite tables. Their long-barreled guns lay on the table before them, causing waves of fear throughout the train. During the night we arrived at Culiacán where the whole group left the train. They were caught up in a surge of thousands of white-clad peons brandishing torches in a tumultuous welcome.

As the train moved away from the massive demonstration, tension subsided. At the border we declared our purchases, only to have the pelican pelt confiscated as contraband. There, to our relief, the little red car waited to take us back to Taliesin.

After our return from Mexico, Peter, a good builder with an excellent sense of design, built a desert tent "Triptych" near the mountain. Built on a wooden platform, two tents and a high stone fireplace dominated the points of a triangle. The openings between the units framed views of the mountains and valley. One tent had two bed platforms with space between for a two-burner Coleman stove. The other tent served as storage and wardrobe.

Often at night we heard the calls of coyotes and mountain lions or felt the tents shake when wild horses brushed by. Peter had a succession of cats who hunted. Their trophies, dead squirrels and half-eaten jackrabbits, usually appeared under our beds.

Our tent Triptych had a special charm on cold winter nights when the fire in our fireplace sent sparks to the stars and gave heat to our tents. Also, the Coleman lantern hanging from the apex of the tent reflected warmth and a glowing light for reading.

Since I was pregnant that winter, crawling out of bed on cold dark mornings was not easy. Nevertheless I took my turn cooking breakfast, which meant getting up at four o'clock and making my way through cactus to the camp with the aid of a flashlight. One such morning I had just started breakfast when my kitchen helper appeared with a strange looking young man. Thinking the man to

Triptych desert tent built by Peter Berndtson

be his guest, I gave them coffee and asked a few polite questions. "Where are you from?" etc. The man, reluctant to answer, finally mumbled that he came from the east and intended to go to find his sister in California. Bolting his coffee, he thanked me, hurried out to the point of the terrace and disappeared in the darkness. My helper explained that although it had been raining all night, the man had appeared in the locker room looking perfectly dry. Later we figured out he must have come over the mountains, escaping from something, and spent the night in camp. At that time our uninhabited land of cactus could swallow any convict, especially on a dark winter morning.

Spring arrival

When spring came, Peter and I drove to Pittsburgh to visit my aunts who had started building the house Mr. Wright helped me design. The house was nearing completion, but the contractor was defaulting on so many scores that Peter and I stayed to supervise and finally took over the job. The young contractor began forging signatures, which resulted in my aunts paying twice for labor and materials. They could have sent the young fellow to jail but didn't have the heart to do so.

We arrived there in April 1940, with ground still covered in snow, but, being conditioned to the outdoor life, we pitched our tent on the building site. In June as the house neared completion, Mr. Wright came to visit. He asked us to drive him to Mars, Pennsylvania, home of the Bantam cars. Although I expected my baby at any moment, Mr. Wright insisted I go along. Since the Fellowship already had a fleet of these miniature, Cherokee-red Bantam cars, I don't remember the exact reason for the trip. We arrived back in Pittsburgh just in time to put Mr. Wright on the seven o'clock evening train. The next morning at seven o'clock I went to the hospital. Our first baby girl arrived that evening.

Cozy accommodations

85

Our daughter's birth became such an event for our friends at Taliesin that everyone began to suggest names. Peter, thinking of his Swedish roots, wanted to call her Brunhilda, a name I thought too long for a baby. If the baby had been a boy I wanted to call him Sven. So when a beautiful little girl appeared, I said, "Why not Svenya?"

Mrs. Wright was horrified. "Svenya?" she said. "It means pig in five languages." So Svenya was out. We returned to Taliesin with the baby, and the debate went on for five weeks. Finally, Mr. Wright said, "I'm going to name that baby. I'll call her Anna in honor of my mother." And so, one Sunday evening, at a musical in the living room, he carried her around the room and said, "I christen this baby Anna Berndtson. Has anyone any objections or corrections?"

Peter said, "Mr. Wright, I'd like to call her Anna Brita Berndtson." "No," said Mr. Wright, "that's too much name for a baby. She's going to be Anna Berndtson." And so she is. Mr. Wright always seemed to have a soft spot for our little girl.

The constant pull

Taliesin had always been home to me. Wherever I am away from the Fellowship some magnet, some indefinable current tugs at my being until I return to Taliesin. But Peter wanted to establish his own architectural practice.

During World War II we lived in Spokane, Washington, as Peter worked on plans for secret buildings at Pasco. We later learned the atomic bomb had been developed there. While in Spokane, I designed and made a tufted rug for Taliesin. Here is Mr. Wright's response after receiving it:

Peter with Indira and Anna, 1943

Dear Cornelia: We were really glad to hear from you and receive a
tangible proof of your consideration and ability too.   I have said that
you of all the girls coming to Taliesin got most out of it in spirit and
in deed.   I like the rug very much. And I had always intended to make
you captain of a follow-up brigade to furnish the Usonian houses and house-
break the owners to occupy them gracefully and comfortably.   But the babies
came along too soon for our economy.

Heigh-ho ! . .My best to Peter - I hope his individual creative impulse is
thriving - and of course love to my little Anna, I named her for my mother.

(But why women want to bring children into this world before certain things are str
straightened out, I can't see.)

Best wishes for the happiness of you all -

Frank Lloyd Wright

TALIESIN:SPRING GREEN:WISCONSIN   June 12th, 1942

Peter Berndtson, 1941

Our second baby girl came along while we were in Spokane. We named her Indira, influenced by Jawaharlal Nehru's book, *Glimpses of World History.* When both girls were in their early teens, our East Indian students told Indira her name meant "Goddess of Rain and Emotions." She boasted so much about her romantic name that we had to keep reassuring Anna of her own incredibly important one.

I couldn't wait to return to Taliesin again in 1943. The war had greatly reduced the number of young people, as all of our able-bodied young people, except a few exempted to work on the farm, went to war or into prison as conscientious objectors. The small remaining Taliesin family welcomed us home, and we plunged into work.

Mr. Wright appreciated Peter's help. He had developed into an exceptional artist and draftsman. When the commission for the Guggenheim Museum came to Taliesin, Peter did the first watercolor rendering of it and many other drawings.

We stayed at Taliesin for just three or four years when Peter again became anxious to go out on his own and accepted an offer to return to Pittsburgh to build fourteen houses on the property that had belonged to my aunt. The prospect was exciting to me also, but when leaving Taliesin I couldn't stop crying. We often returned to visit and saw Mr. and Mrs. Wright many times in New York. Ten years later I returned to Taliesin to stay permanently.

Even though our lives in Pennsylvania were full of activity, my whole being yearned to get back to Taliesin. Peter preferred to pursue his practice and refused to go back. Finally I slipped away, never to return.

Playmates

At that time, Taliesin had six children about the same age. Tal Davison, Brandoch Peters, Peter and Eric Drake, and Indira and Anna Berndtson. Playing sometimes got rough, and they went through a period of biting each other. One day, Eric came whining and crying to his mother, "Tal bit me!" My sister Hulda said, "Well, Eric, why don't you bite him back." Eric said, "I can't." Three-year-old Indira came steaming around the corner, full of the old nick. "Eric, I'll bite him!" she said, with real anticipation.

Indira, my youngest daughter, and Wes Peters' son, Brandoch, are about the same age. When they were about three, they played around the Taliesin court-yard in the crunching snow. Both wad-dled about in their clumsy snow suits and boots. I heard Brandoch screaming. He'd fallen face down in the snow. Indira sat on his back, pounding him with a croquet mallet.

Later that year in Arizona, I was cooking in the kitchen when Mrs. Wright came rushing in, furiously push-ing a screaming Brandoch ahead of her, keeping a strong hold on his collar. She

Playing in the pools at Taliesin West
Left to right: (in the pool) Anna Berndtson, Indira Berndtson, Eric Drake
(outside of the pool) Blaine Drake, Peter Drake

shoved him in front of me shouting, "Hit him! Just hit him!" Brandoch screamed and kicked. It was impossible for me to hit him without a reason. Later I found out that Brandoch had managed to get

Brandoch Peters and Tal Davison, 1945

Indira's head in a vice between his legs, pounding it with a rock. The score was even!

They all played together in the pools. The sun made Indira very blond, very tan, and very cute in her bathing suit. Mr. Wright used to watch her with pleasure, calling her, "butter ball," which she resented to the point of refusing to eat butter. He also remarked that she had "a cute profile all the way down."

When the children went out to play we dressed them in their bathing suits. But usually they discarded them and six little nudes would be splashing each other with delight. They referred to the gold fish in the pool as "the fish with the trimmings."

Once, Anna came crying, saying, "Misser Wright won't take me to town." I said, "Do you mean, Mrs. Wright?"

"No," bawled Anna. "I mean the boy that lives in the house." She was referring, of course, to Mr. Wright.

In most respects, growing up at Taliesin is no different than growing up anywhere else. But it is different in one important way. The children are surrounded by "extended family" every day and are included in all aspects of life at Taliesin, from community meals to festivals and parties and even in the work life. This made for rich experiences while growing up.

The lesson

When the Taliesin children were between the ages of three and five we took them to Madison, Wisconsin, for Suzuki lessons. With their miniature fiddles and cellos, they enjoyed their Madison excursion. But one autumn day I took them to their lesson, and on the way home we had a difficult, but life learning, experience.

That evening the Fellowship enjoyed a formal dinner in the theater. The room glowed with the radiance of a great log fire and decorative arrangements of scarlet and golden maple leaves. All our friends, elegantly dressed for the occasion—the men in tuxedos and the ladies in colorful evening gowns—presented a scene of peace and beauty. Mr. Wright's sister Jane Porter and her husband Andrew participated with many other guests.

Mr. Wright was proud of the fact that the children were taking music lessons. He said, "Cornelia, tell us about the trip to Madison."

"We had a harrowing experience," I responded.

What do you mean?" he asked.

"The lessons came off well," I said, "but we had real trouble on the way home. I'm still completely upset! As we drove along quietly Anna suddenly asked, 'Mother, what is a library?' I told her, 'It's a place where books are kept, where people can go to read.' 'No,' she said emphatically, 'I don't mean that! What is a library?' Suddenly I realized we had just passed the cemetery near Mazomanie. 'Do you mean the cemetery that we just passed?' 'Yes, What is that?' 'Oh,' I said, grasping for a way to break the information, 'when people die their spirit travels to God, but their body is no longer useful and is buried in the

Two young families: the Drakes (Cornelia's sister, Hulda, and brother-in-law, Blaine, with Peter and Eric) and the Berndtsons (Cornelia, Peter, Anna, Indira), 1943

ground.' The children began to cry. Stricken with the awful thought of burial, they all sobbed. Anna demanded through her sobs, 'Tell me something good that God does.' In anguish, I said, 'He makes the beautiful flowers, the forests, the clouds, and the sun.' 'No,' demanded Anna, 'I mean something good!' 'Well,' I said, 'He made Brandoch's little brother, Daniel. Perhaps Daniel at one time was another person who died but God sent him back to be Brandoch's brother.' The children stopped crying immediately. Brandoch puffed out his chest and patted it, 'Daniel,' he said proudly, 'that's my brother!' The children were all delighted about Daniel's reappearance and sun shone again in the car."

"What a good story," Mr. Wright said. But his sister Jane was furious. "I think Cornelia did a terrible thing, Frank; how dare she teach reincarnation to those little children."

Mr. Wright said, "Jane, I think it was a wonderful way to give the children hope." "Nonsense!" Jane exploded.

A typical Lloyd Jones brouhaha ensued between Mr. Wright and sister Jane. The verbal battle raged until Jane rose to her full height, marched to the door and said, "Come on Andrew. We're leaving!" The peace of the autumn evening was shattered.

Eric Lloyd Wright and Brandoch Peters, Mr. Wright's grandsons.

A party at the Sun Trap

In 1941, Peter and I lived in the "Sun Trap," a charming, colorful desert fantasy, built with three sleeping boxes. These were arranged in a U-shape at one end of the enclosed terrace. Each box was just large enough for a built-in bed, a four-foot-square closet and a small desk that separated the bed from the terrace. The wooden box was covered with tan canvas. The bedspreads and pillows were of red, purple, turquoise, and yellow canvas—each box being distinguished by a different color. Designed in two levels, a canvas trellis extended over the central part of the terrace. The rest of the terrace was unroofed, with a large stone fireplace in one corner. Strings of colored gourds and red peppers hung from the trellis, and Native American pots and rugs abounded.

One evening Peter and I gave a party for Llewellyn and Betty Wright, Mr. Wright's son and daughter-in-law, and their two boys, Timmy, aged four, and Tom, aged six. During that day, the boys had played havoc with the men's tools by using newly sharpened saws to work on the stone parapets and by throwing tools into the pool. Marcus Weston, an apprentice from Spring Green, defended them saying, "I think they're nice little fellows." With Marcus' help the boys were lifting buckets of water from the pool. Struggling with their heavy loads, they kept making trips around the corner. Finally Marcus went to see where all the water was going. To his horror he saw his keg of nails filled with water to the brim. At that moment his kindly protectionism vanished.

During the day, Mrs. Wright felt that Betty Wright needed a break and asked me to take care of them for awhile. All afternoon Tim, Tom, and I sat in the sun on the terrace, stringing colored beads and small squares of white leather to make necklaces for Betty. The boys were completely absorbed in the project. When Betty arrived, she appeared to be thunderstruck at the beautiful results. She couldn't believe the boys had sat still long enough to make the necklaces.

That night at the party the boys sat quietly, though good behavior was not exactly their style. In order to entertain them, we gathered around a blazing, spirited fire that sent sparks high into the starry night. While singing "Polly Wolly Doodle," someone said, "Alfie, give us a dance. A dance, Alfie!" Alfie Bush, a sturdy, muscular young fellow from Brooklyn who had danced with Danny Kaye, stripped to the waist, and danced in the firelight until his bronzed muscles glistened. With the clapping of the audience, his impromptu performance to "Polly Wolly Doodle" was spectacular.

Betty and Llewellyn planned to leave the next day. As they were about to depart in their car, someone noticed dollar bills sticking out of Timmy's pockets. He had raided Svetlana's Indian basket that held her cash, but he was too young a bandit to make off with the loot.

Packrats and skunks

In the desert we've had intimate experiences with animals, especially packrats and skunks. When Mildred and I lived in an open shelter, we were prime targets for their activities. Sometimes, packrats stole our shiny earrings, replacing them with pebbles. To retrieve the stolen goods, we had to hunt through packrat nests of cholla balls, which in itself is a precarious business. We usually emerged with painful punctures from the barbed spines. Then all would be peaceful until the next episode.

One night it became apparent that a packrat had built a nest under my cot. I was wakened by the squeaking of baby rats. I couldn't sleep so I took my sleeping bag outside for the rest of the night. The next morning Kevin Lynch, a dedicated pacifist, using a shovel, moved the rat family to some distance from the shelter. In the middle of the night, the family returned to its home under my cot. Again, Kevin removed them, this time to a greater distance, but sure enough, they returned. After that, in

Llewellyn Wright with Tommy and Timmy

desperation, I begged Kevin to destroy them. I suppose he did, as all through the next night, I suffered the agony of hearing the mother rat squeaking and running in circles under my bed.

Throughout our life in tents we endured episodes of packrat invasions. When I was married to Peter, we lived in a suite of rooms around the Apprentice Court. Each room had a bank of wardrobes on one side, and in the fall when we returned from Wisconsin, the wardrobes would be chock full of cholla balls from floor to ceiling—a sort of condominium for packrats. Shoveling them out was a messy job, and always, as we got to the bottom we would find a skunk, for rats' nests are favorite feeding grounds for skunks.

These desert skunks are smaller and more attractive than their northern counterpart, but since they didn't seem to be afraid of us, we couldn't get them to leave. We tried smoking them out. No luck! Then, one time, Peter decided to guide one out of the room with a broom handle. First he laid a low wall of boards to direct the skunk to the door. He gently eased the skunk out of its lair, directing it carefully. All went well but just before it got to the door, it lifted its bushy tail and let Peter have it

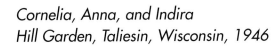

Cornelia, Anna, and Indira
Hill Garden, Taliesin, Wisconsin, 1946

Indira Berndtson

Anna Berndtson and
Roger Coor

in the face. That night, our baby daughter Indira, who had watched this performance, was sleeping in a screened crib and called, "Mother, Mother, there's a skunk in my bed!"

"No, Indira, there can't be."

"Yes, there is!" I turned on the light, and lifted the screened lid. Indira sat up in bed, looked astonished, and said, "He's gone!"

At one time we had two tame skunks that came to eat in the dining room when we were having dinner. They had their own dish in one corner of the room. But tragedy struck! One night, a roasted turkey was left in the oven. One of the skunks went down the vent into the oven and gorged on the turkey. He got so fat from the feast that he couldn't get back up the vent. In the morning, an unsuspecting breakfast cook turned on the oven. When he opened it to put in a pan of biscuits, he found a depleted turkey and our poor, fat, roasted pet skunk!

Packrats and skunk episodes have become less frequent now around the buildings. With the influx of many people, the animals have retreated further into the desert, but our tent dwellers can still tell stories of close encounters.

Iovanna Wright as a young girl, 1936

TALES OF MY OWN

Iovanna

After I'd been at Taliesin a short time, Mrs. Wright asked me to teach their daughter Iovanna reading and arithmetic, as Mr. Wright, for reasons of his own, refused to have her go to school. This became a matter of a novice trying to teach a novice. Iovanna and I sat in her sunlit room struggling over our mutual problem. What emerged from our sessions did not turn into much of an academic accomplishment, but a genuine mutual friendship developed. Consequently, we took many walks in the woods and fields.

Besides having a brilliant mind, Iovanna had become an excellent horsewoman. Her youth (then about seven or eight years old) and her small stature belied her capacity for command, and the horses knew it. I had never ridden a horse, so Iovanna decided to teach me. She picked out a gentle horse for me, and we started up the road. She drew alongside and, with great kindness and affection, explained how to hold the reins and how to sit.

All of my timidity, confusion, and awkwardness must have gotten to her as she pulled far ahead, and although she tried to conceal her mirth, there was no doubt that she doubled over with laughter. I never became comfortable with horses. When I walked beside them, they tried to bite me, so I preferred our walks to our horseback sessions.

The reading lessons continued, but Mrs. Wright was very serious about getting Iovanna to school. One day she called me into the little dining room where she and Mr. Wright were having an argument about the subject. Mr. Wright insisted that learning to write was unimportant. Mrs. Wright said, "What do you think, Cornelia?" I said, "I think it would be impossible for an architect to implement his plans without writing explanations." This seemed to make an impression on Mr. Wright and, with further prodding from Mrs. Wright, he finally agreed that Iovanna should attend school.

Beginning school at such a late age made life very difficult for Iovanna since she lagged far behind the children of her age group. After her solitary childhood among all the adults at Taliesin, she did not find making friends with other children easy. To this day, I don't understand why Mr. Wright was so adamant about not wanting Iovanna to attend school. But in spite of a difficult beginning, she became an excellent writer and poet.

Later, after studying with Gurdjieff, Iovanna began conducting exercises in correlations. These exercises, taught to her by Gurdjieff, were mainly based on ancient Asiatic rituals designed to coordinate mind, body, and spirit. Iovanna with her great creative energy wove these and other exercises that she choreographed into scripts for dance dramas for public performance. These in-depth scenarios engaged the talents of the entire Fellowship. Mrs. Wright wrote the dance music—played by the Phoenix Symphony—and, together with Iovanna, supervised making costumes,

the lighting, and creation of stage sets. These performances marked a high point in creativity and Fellowship cooperation.

In August 1987, Iovanna sent me a letter, from which I quote in part:

These early woodland adventures with Iovanna are now treasured memories of an unusual companionship.

Do you remember long years ago—in a past that can never pass—a young woman and a child used to take walks together. They were you and me. I was about 7, and somehow I guess you took a shine to me—asking me for walks, reading, and telling me stories, all of which I loved. . . . We sat down at the river's edge—the young woman told the tow-headed child a story. . . . They got up, carrying their shoes, and moved deep, nearly to the center of the leaning trees. And there, growing from the soft, gentle earth, the only one of her kind for miles around her, was a wild, yellow Lady Slipper. The child knew that she was watching real magic. . . .

"Do you think the Lady Slipper is lonely, Cornelia?"

"No. She has the long grasses and the trees to talk to."

"Would she speak to me, do you think?"

"No. Not now. I bet she speaks as the sun goes down. And maybe other Lady Slippers are growing—so quietly."

The little child did not know that one day she would wear golden slippers. And the companion did not yet know that her sense of beauty was gold in her hands.

Presenting Broadacre City

After building the Broadacre City model at Chandler during the spring of 1935, we returned to Wisconsin. In the summer it fell to my lot to show the model in Pittsburgh and Washington, D.C. Kaufmann's Department Store featured Broadacre City in Pittsburgh, where I spoke to thousands of visitors every day, trying my best to explain Mr. Wright's idea for decentralization, which he felt was bound to happen with the increasing numbers of cars and trucks. Therefore, he thought it necessary to start some long-range planning.

The ideas stimulated the imagination of those who came to listen. City managers, editors, engineers, and others came to take notes, which later led to many of the decentralized features of our present life. At that time, a series of local roads joined together comprised the very minimal Lincoln Highway, which wound its narrow way across America. Mr. Wright proposed an expanded freeway with separate lanes for cars and trucks, with a monorail train in the center. He suggested warehouses could be put under the highway so that large trucks could unload there and let smaller conveyances carry the freight throughout the area.

Broadacre City model on display at the Corcoran Gallery

Land use assumed the utmost importance for the populace—at least an acre per person with workshops or offices in the home. No time should be spent traveling to and from work. Markets should be decentralized, and motels represented important features at a time when most travelers stayed with families who took tourists into their homes. The ideas of Broadacre City influenced city planning throughout the United States and Europe.

After the Pittsburgh exhibition closed, Mr. Wright drove me from there to the Corcoran Gallery in Washington, stopping on the way at the future site of the Kaufmann house, Fallingwater, which had just been commissioned. That marvelous site, with dashing stream and falls and lush foliage of rhododendrons and hemlocks, dogwood, red bud, chestnuts, oaks, tulip trees, sassafras, and more. This poetic site greatly inspired Mr. Wright. What more exciting spot could he find for such complete integration of house with existent, exuberant, native foliage and scenery.

A survey once made by an Austrian Commission studying all the foliage of the United States, determined that that area of Pennsylvania mountains contained the greatest variety of foliage of any area of the country. Being a great student of nature, Mr. Wright advised native landscaping and spacious sites beyond city congestion wherever possible.

But on to the Corcoran Gallery, where all visitors came by appointment. Mrs. Eleanor Roosevelt, interested in Broadacre City, sent her press secretary, Sigrid Anne, of the Associated Press, to interview me. Senators and congressmen, many foreign dignitaries, and engineers kept me on my toes with questions. The sweltering summer left the shirts of the men always limp and wet, but my enthusiasm never dampened.

Interesting hosts

While in Washington, Mr. Parma, who headed the Rare Book Room of the Library of Congress, and his wife, took me under their wing. They considered Mr. Wright a great seer and thought his ideas should be part of some vast, cosmic plan for which they had been working.

They believed that an unknown final calamity would occur and felt they had been chosen to consolidate a plan of survival involving many groups of people and including the supply authorities of the army, navy, and so on.

The Parmas experimented with and investigated all sorts of supernatural phenomena, including the study of the dematerialization of metals. They claimed that in their studies of the supernatural, they asked for enlightenment, and, while Mrs. Parma played the harp, all things were revealed to them. They lived in a fascinating old Washington house, with rooms and gardens on many levels. Their two small, blind poodles had to be carried up and down steps from room to room.

During my stay, the Parmas took me to the Library of Congress to see the Rare Book Room, which housed marvelous old illuminated manuscripts. I noticed one volume bound in human skin, with marks of the vertebrae on the back. Thinking of this place revives for me memories of the bizarre and the beautiful.

Traveling with the Broadacre City model opened many doors and provided experiences and opportunities that I would otherwise never have had. Fifty years after we completed the model,

Indira and I travelled to Paris where a French museum included Broadacre City as a centerpiece of an exhibit on ideas of land use planning.

Ahead of his time

With the passing of years, many of Mr. Wright's predictions and ideas for Broadacre City have come to pass. The worldwide network of super highways, the wayside markets that have developed into suburban malls with shops and entertainment facilities, and the wide distribution of motels and suburban housing have dominated contemporary land use pattern. Town planning, which was in its infancy during the 1930s, has become an accepted necessity for cities nationwide. Other aspects of his ideas have not taken hold, and planners, as a consequence, now have to deal with sprawl instead of well-defined and well-designed communities. As Mr. Wright suggested, more people now work at home, a possibility that came about with the advent of computers. Architects and planners still study the Broadacre City model as a viable thesis for decentralization.

Broadacre City model, 1935

Broadacre City model

The hexagonal unit

The following spring of 1936 the Taliesin Fellowship once again headed for Arizona and the Hacienda in Chandler. Several clients commissioned Mr. Wright to design houses. One request came from Mr. and Mrs. Paul Hanna. Mr. Wright suggested each apprentice select a house and try his hand at designing. I saw Mr. Wright experimenting with the hexagonal unit for furniture. The idea of fitting pieces together in a honeycomb pattern intrigued him. Taking a cue from his work, I decided to use a hexagonal unit for the Hanna house plan.

When Mr. Wright saw the hexagonal unit being used, he became completely absorbed with the possibilities for the extension of space by way of the obtuse angles. As always, when presented with a new idea Mr. Wright immediately explored its possibilities. His final plan for the Hannas showed no trace of my amateurish beginning, but he always gave me credit for initiating the hexagon for the Hanna's house.

Later, when I tried to use a rectangular unit for my aunts' house, the Notz house, Mr. Wright said, "No, Cornelia. No rectangle. Your unit is the hexagonal unit."

Snow in the desert

In the winter of 1992 it snowed in the desert. Big snow flakes drifted over the cactus and left the desert floor and the mountains white. The weatherman pronounced it the first big snow since 1939. Nineteen thirty-nine! How well I remember that snow.

In 1939 I lived in an Arabian-style tent near the mountain. The night turned unusually cold, but I went to bed feeling snug in my tent with the canvas floor, a window with a flap to tie shut, a canvas door that also tied shut to keep out the drafts, and a charcoal brazier to keep things warm.

During the night I woke up feeling desperate for air. Being extremely hot, I tried unsuccessfully to untie the window flap. In a semi-conscious state, I tried to get to the door but collapsed between my cot and the brazier. Bodily functions were out of control, but the brazier burned me. I became conscious enough to drag myself to the door. It was tied shut with several knotted straps. With great mental and physical effort, I slowly untied one knot after another. By holding onto the edge of the canvas, I gradually pulled myself up and stood in the freezing air.

Snowflakes drifted around me. Somehow, in my dazed state, it seemed that I would be all right if I could just see the saguaro about ten feet away. I broke the ice on my wash basin and dashed ice water over my fiery skin. Finally, I came to enough to see the outline of the saguaro. In the tent the brazier glowed. White hot coals had burned all the oxygen. The canvas that usually breathed such a healthy circulation of air had been sealed by the wet snowflakes.

By the grace of the Gods I survived that desert snowstorm. Nineteen thirty-nine!

Home again

My return to Taliesin from my years in Pennsylvania was a healing balm. After the constraints of marriage, the release of pent-up emotions overwhelmed me. The best possible solution came as I plunged into the varied activities of the Fellowship. Mrs. Wright suggested I become shopper for a complete change of activity, after having lived a more-or-less sedentary life in our studio in Pennsylvania. So, during the summer in Wisconsin I drove to Madison every day for groceries, produce, and decorating and building materials. When in

Arizona, I shopped in Phoenix at the Farmer's Market and wholesale houses.

About this time I had a minor operation. One night in Arizona, during recovery, while wearing my robe and sitting in my room at the desk a storm raged outside. Every flash of lightning revealed rain-swept bushes and cactus. Suddenly the door banged open. A torrent of water gushed into the room. Within a matter of seconds I waded in water a foot deep and rising. "Help! Help!" I screamed.

As I frantically pulled clothes from the closet and put them on the desk, Herbert Hughes, an apprentice, plunged into the room. Laughing hysterically, he gleefully "helped" drag loads of evening dresses through the water and piled them in a soggy mess on the desk. Out in the gravel courtyard people sloshed through knee-deep water, trying to open drainage areas.

Sudden floods come to the desert during the monsoon season. Water cascades down from the mountains pouring over the hard, sun-baked surface of the slopes. The drainage ditches above the buildings immediately overflow and the unimpeded flood pours over walls, terraces and rooms. Walls of water send boulders crashing down the dry washes to the valley below, where in the early years before the area became built up,

Brahmin cattle lazily browsed dry grass around creosote bushes. When flooded at that time, the valley became an impossible lake. For two or three days, until the water subsided, I could do no shopping in Phoenix or Scottsdale.

Trucking

For a few years, I spent most of my time doing the daily shopping for Taliesin. Generally, I drove a pickup, sometimes an old Dodge car, an old Oldsmobile, or a van. Because of numerous incidents of losing things from the load, I became experienced in securing things on the truck.

One time, buying a load of plywood that stuck out over the back of the pickup, I asked the man loading it to tie it so it wouldn't slide off. He gave me a deprecating look and said, "Lady, that plywood is so heavy it can't slide!" But going up a slight rise at an intersection, the whole load shuffled off and spread over the highway. Heavy traffic lines formed in all directions. Being unable to lift the sheets of plywood, I tried to get two loafers standing on the curb to help. They shifted from one foot to the other and said "Lady, we ain't liftin' that." By this time, people in the cars honked and cursed. Finally, just in order to be able to

proceed, some of the drivers gathered up the broadcast plywood and put it back on the truck. The police arrived to unscramble the traffic jam, and in utter humiliation I drove on back to Taliesin.

During the early years, Phoenix had a farmers' market. In order to buy the best produce, getting there at four in the morning was desirable. Farmers came from as far away as Yuma. Their trucks, laden with chard, peppers, cabbage, melons, etc., encircled the market area. The men became my friends, and after making purchases I had breakfast in the market restaurant where, I being the only woman, everyone treated me with great courtesy.

One day, driving the old Dodge touring car, I filled the back seat with vegetables, topping off the load with a garnish of turnips. By the time I started home the heavy traffic was in full flow. When we came to a sudden stop in an intersection of Camelback Road, I tramped on the brake. Crash! The transmission fell out of the car. All the turnips fell forward and festooned my head and neck with greens. People in the cars beside me couldn't help laughing but came to my rescue by pushing the car into a gas station.

Truckloads varied from produce to groceries, to plate glass, lumber, plumbing equipment, party decorations, and all other necessities for our varied life. We often bought tanks of helium used to fill balloons, gas for welding, etc. Once, starting for the market on a cold winter morning, Joe Fabris said, "There's a tank in the van to be returned downtown. Just give it to the night watchman." Driving across the desert on such a cold night is a lonely experience. A coyote trotted across the road. The tank began to bang from one side of the van to the other, loosening the valve. Blue smoke filled the van. Driving to town as fast as possible, I pulled into an all-night gas station where I jumped out to ask the owner's help. "Get that damn thing out of here!" he bellowed. In fear of blowing up, I climbed back in and backed the van into the street. The air filled with blue smoke. Seeing was difficult. I had visions of gas not only blowing up but also poisoning me.

The station attendant, who thought I didn't move the car fast enough, grudgingly let me use his phone to call the night watchman to ask advice. When it was explained how the valve could be tightened, I gingerly climbed into the cab, held my breath, felt for the valve, and turned it off. With shattered nerves, I drove to town to deliver the tank. When the watchman inspected it, he said, "Nothing dangerous, just oxygen!"

At another time, the seat of my Volkswagen station wagon seemed to be jammed, and it wouldn't push back. Holding the lever under the seat, I lunged back as hard as I could. Immediately, there was a terrific explosion. White smoke filled the car. Stranded on the road, I tried to imagine what had happened. Taliesin member Arnold Roy fortunately came by. "Simple," he said. "You punctured the fire extinguisher."

Today I happily leave truck driving to our younger apprentices, who are being trained in purchasing materials and groceries.

Dark day at Taliesin

Mr. Wright, nearing his ninety-second birthday in April 1959, walked down the pergola at Taliesin West, swinging his cane and enjoying the beneficence of a balmy day. Of the two women walking behind me, one said, "They said he's over ninety." "Nonsense," the other visitor said, "He doesn't look a day over sixty-five."

Because Mr. Wright always looked so well, his death came as a great shock to all of us. I woke up very early one morning to a great stillness everywhere. My waking vision (one that I am powerless to describe) seemed to be of some divine presence "bearing up" Mr. and Mrs. Wright. The phone rang. Gene Masselink said, "Cornelia, Mr. Wright has just passed away." His death plunged Taliesin into deep, silent sorrow. Mr. Wright's presence seemed to be everywhere.

Reorganization and rededication

Mrs. Wright, though crushed by the blow, rallied with amazing courage to lead the Fellowship into a new era. A total reorganization followed. Previously Mr. Wright had managed all aspects of the studio. As a highly organized person, he did all the designing, building details, specifications, client correspondence, and billing. Also, Mr. Wright handled all finances. Since he didn't have much faith in banks, any available money came directly from his pockets. Sometimes this involved a fist full of crumpled checks or just whatever cash he had on hand.

Senior members, able and distinguished men who had worked closely with Mr. Wright for years by implementing drawings, working on engineering and supervising buildings, registered for architectural licenses. John deKoven Hill (whom we called Johnny) returned from *House Beautiful* magazine as editorial director for ten years, where he had been "on loan" from Taliesin. He became secretary of The Frank Lloyd Wright Foundation. The board of directors included Mrs. Wright as president and Wes Peters as vice president. Mr. Wright had set up The Frank Lloyd Wright Foundation in 1940, giving to it all of his intellectual and personal property. He confirmed this in his will, and the Foundation, with Mrs. Wright at its head, took over the direction of Taliesin and Mr. Wright's architectural practice.

Before Johnny returned from *House Beautiful*, Mrs. Wright sent me as emissary to help clients with their interior furnishings. Since she had an unusual sense of color, Mrs. Wright set the tone for many interiors. The house for Frank and Eloise Bott in Kansas City needed furnishing. Good fortune gave me an opportunity to buy beautiful fabrics and objects of art, including fine Japanese screens.

I also had the pleasure of furnishing the Stromquist house in Bountiful, Utah. I saw by the distinguished clothes Mrs. Stromquist wore that she had a lovely color sense. We worked together to select appealing fabrics for the house. Later, because Mr. Stromquist's company transferred him to another city they had to sell the house. It fell into the unworthy hands of a man who kept horses in the living room.

Fortunately, just recently, George Frandsen and David Carlquist bought the house. After doing a remarkable job of restoration, they called on me to refurnish the home. Since Johnny and I now worked together, we both enjoyed bringing the present interior alive by remaking some of the original furniture and selecting a luxurious carpet and fabrics that compliment this crystalline woodland home.

As the years have gone by, there has been no tapering off of architectural commissions, as our senior architects were already well known and their talents appreciated.

Contemporaries in spirit

During my years at Taliesin, I worked many times with Mr. Wright in decorating the Fellowship rooms. When we needed samples of carpets, fabrics, plastics, or paint colors, Mr. Wright sent me shopping. And so it came about that I found many of decorating materials for buildings such as the Beth Shalom Synagogue in Philadelphia and the Guggenheim Museum in New York. Mr. Wright, usually pleased with the samples I found, discussed the possibilities with very enlightening comments. Mr. Wright was always partial to me, from the time I joined Taliesin until the last years of his life.

Once in Arizona, in the late fifties, we endured a plague of nasty black caterpillars that crawled over the floors, walls, ceilings, and, of course, the gardens. Finally, they emerged as small reddish brown butterflies. One day Mr. Wright and I stood in the garden enjoying the myriads of butterflies dancing in the sunlight around us. We had a moment of mutual appreciation. Mr. Wright, some forty-five years older than I, said, "Cornelia, you and I are contemporaries." His whole conversation led me to suspect that he considered us as of one age. Mr. Wright had the quality of entering into and enjoying the youthful spirit of any moment.

Mr. Wright improvising at the piano

Mr. and Mrs. Wright, 1956

Olgivanna Lloyd Wright

A

Taliesin, Wisconsin

Tea Circle, Taliesin, Wisconsin

Taliesin entrance court

B

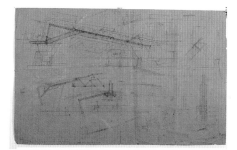

Original Taliesin West detail drawing on brown craft paper by Frank Lloyd Wright

Taliesin West, Winter 1939

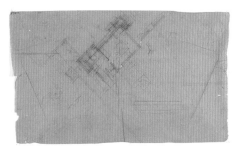

Original Taliesin West detail drawing on brown craft paper by Frank Lloyd Wright

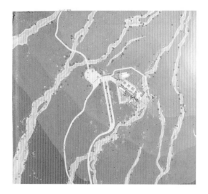

Taliesin West, Spring 1998

Painting of Taliesin West original building site

C

Taliesin West

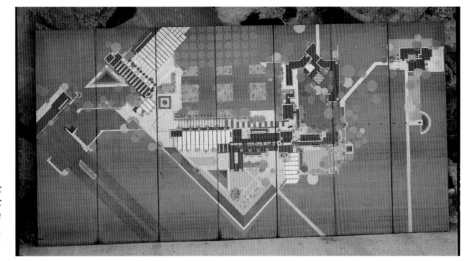

Painted panel of original site plan of Taliesin West that still stands in the living room

D

Dance drama performance

Mary Magdalene
Heloise Crista (standing), Susan Lockhart (kneeling)

Hillside Theatre interior view of curtain, Taliesin, Wisconsin

E

*Easter celebration balloons
tied together*

The baba and pascha cheese

Sending Easter balloons aloft

Easter breakfast on the terrace, 1953

F

The Pearl Palace in Iran

Interior scenes of the Pearl Palace

G

TALIESEN FELLOWSHIP — 60th REUNION
Sept. 10-13, 1992   Spring Green, WI

Cornelia is standing in the center of the second row

PARTNERS IN ADVENTURE

Many exceptionally talented people have come to Taliesin. When Mr. and Mrs. Wright formed the Fellowship in 1932, Jack Howe, first to come and an excellent draftsman, became the "pencil in Mr. Wright's hand." Jack saw to the completion of many working drawings. He left during the early sixties for private practice. Other early arrivals, Edgar Tafel and Bob Moser, contributed to work in the studio but left in the early forties to establish their own offices.

Especially gifted ones who came in the thirties and stayed to devote their entire lives to further the cause of Mr.

Snapping beans. Cornelia is on the far right sipping tea with Indira standing in front of Mr. Wright and Anna sitting on the floor at the far left

Informal Fellowship gathering at Taliesin West, 1942

Wright's work and the Fellowship were Wes Peters, Gene Masselink, John deKoven Hill, Kenn Lockhart, and Davy Davison—all men of genius, each with different aptitudes. Having weathered the Second World War, Dick Carney arrived. His executive talents carried the work of the Frank Lloyd Wright Foundation into the future. Bruce Pfeiffer, also of genius status, came later and became responsible for establishing Mr. Wright's internationally important archives. Bruce has authored many books to disseminate the treasure of the archives for world study. Ling Po, having escaped the Chinese Revolution, gave his boundless creative talents to every aspect of Taliesin life. He has recently retreated to a Buddhist monastery.

Other architects and other partners who are still carrying on important work in all aspects of Taliesin life are Charles Montooth, Joe Fabris, Arnold Roy, Tom Casey, John Rattenbury, David Dodge, and Stephen Nemtin. Over the years the number of people that have contributed and then gone worldwide to practice architecture are legion. They include such fine architects as John Lautner, Fay Jones, and Aaron Green, our San Francisco associate. Other great spirits, too numerous to mention, have a special niche in Taliesin folklore.

Although all their full stories are not presented here, I would be remiss not to mention the highly developed women of Taliesin and the many strengths they have contributed throughout the years. Heloise Crista is recognized nationally as a fine sculptor; Frances Nemtin, as an exceptional gardener responsible for the continued landscaping of both campuses; Effi Casey, an accomplished musician; Susan Lockhart, a well-known artist and musician; Minerva Montooth, our social coordinator; her artistic twin sister, Sarah Logue; my daughter, Indira Berndtson, head of oral history department of the archives; and Dori Roy, who adds her strength and gentleness to all occasions. Perhaps the story of their complete contribution to the Taliesin Fellowship will be presented later in other volumes, but for now the following abridged versions must suffice.

THE PARTNERS

Richard Carney

Richard Carney joined the Fellowship after World War II. As the son of a Southern Baptist minister, he arrived without funds. Mr. Wright, also the son of a minister, understood his problem and accepted him without tuition. Ever since, Dick has given a good account of himself and repaid Taliesin many times over. As one of his first responsibilities, he took care of Mr. Wright's room, kept his clothes in order, and drove him to his appointments.

It soon became clear that Dick had a great imagination and aptitude for party and set designs in our theater. He created many unusual, inventive effects for our dance performances. One of his most elegant spectaculars was the design for our crystalline Christmas and New Years' parties. Dick, with the help of many apprentices, cut and formed clear plastics into fantastic crystals.

At the parties, we arranged tables in a U-shape to seat 150 guests on the stage of the pavilion (our music and dance theater at Taliesin West). Covered with sky blue cloth and decorated with Italian lights, the tables sparkled under a garland of reflecting crystals. Tall ivory candles completed the decorations and long, many-faceted crystals dangling from the ceiling added to the brilliant design.

To these splendid formal parties Mrs. Wright invited favorite guests—the Henry Luces, the George Ullmans, the William Bentons, the William Wrigleys, and many others.

Mrs. Wright, with her insight into the lives of people, first recognized Dick's talents, including his executive ability. After her death Dick became Chief Executive Officer and President of the Frank Lloyd Wright Foundation as

Richard Carney and Margaret Thatcher, 1997

Mrs. Wright had suggested. Over the years the Foundation has developed into a multifaceted corporation that includes The Frank Lloyd Wright School of Architecture, Taliesin Architects, The Frank Lloyd Wright Archives, visitor and licensing programs, and worldwide exhibitions. For years Dick has devoted his enormous energy to the Foundation to extend Fellowship life into the future.

In 1994 Dick had a battle with lung cancer. With great will throughout chemotherapy treatments he continued his grueling work schedule and air travel back and forth from Spring Green or Scottsdale to treatment in Tucson. With never a hitch in Fellowship management, he overcame the cancer, which went into remission.

Besides the volume of Foundation business Dick has promoted a licensing program by contracting with companies to reproduce some of Mr. Wright's many treasures from the archives in order to make them available to the public. This has involved worldwide travel to Italy, Japan, and other countries.

In 1987 Tommy Thompson, Governor of Wisconsin, realized Taliesin's international renown. He appointed a commission to consider how best to extend the life of Taliesin buildings into the future. From the impetus of that commission's report, Dick helped establish the present Taliesin Preservation Commission, a Wisconsin-based nonprofit corporation which has become a part of our active life. Dedicated admirers of Mr. Wright and the Fellowship contribute support as do many others who appreciate the rewards of visiting these historic buildings.

To help administer the far-flung enterprise Dr. Nicholas Muller, former head of the State Historical Society of Wisconsin, has joined the Foundation to work with Dick. Dr. Muller became President and CEO, and Dick was Chairman of the Board until his death in 1998.

Allen Lape Davison "Davy"

I met Davy in 1938 when I'd gone home to Pittsburgh to visit my aunts. At Mr. Wright's suggestion, Davy came there to be interviewed by me and to inquire about Taliesin. We had an immediate rapport that later developed into a friendship lasting over thirty years. In the last month of Davy's life he said to me: "When I first visited you in Pittsburgh, I thought, as you came down the stairs in that stunning evening dress, that you were the most gorgeous creature I'd ever seen." Flattered but humorously exasperated, I said, "Davy, now you tell me! After thirty years!"

Davy became an exceptionally fine artist and architect. He drew many memorable renderings of Mr. Wright's buildings. One of the most famous is the night scene of the Pittsburgh Point Park Project at the confluence of the Allegheny and the Monongahela Rivers.

A.L. "Davy" Davison

He rendered another of Monona Terrace at night, which, sixty years after Mr. Wright first presented the idea, Madison, Wisconsin completed as the Monona Terrace Convention Center in 1997.

Davy enjoyed life. He had a gleeful sense of humor and could always tell a good joke appropriate to the moment. Our children played together. His son, Tal, and my daughter, Indira, at about age three were found by Kay, Tal's mother, in a closet under the clothes trying to smoke a cigarette. Tal was just as full of the old nick as his father.

Davy's fun-filled skit performances rose to memorable heights. At one costume party he dressed as a girl. He wore my long gold satin evening dress with a train, my high heeled gold pumps, a well-coiffured wig, and seductive makeup. A knockout! As an actress Davy could be as flirtatious as any female. He completely fooled and captivated one of our male guests who continued to make passes at him throughout the evening. All of us, including Mr. and Mrs. Wright, enjoyed his lively humor.

When the war came along, Davy, along with other conscientious objectors, had to go to prison at Sandstone, Minnesota. There, because of Mr. Wright's suggestion to the warden, Davy taught classes in sketching and architecture. Although prison time weighed heavily on such a free spirit, Davy had time to hone his architectural and delineation skills. Upon his return to Taliesin he made invaluable contributions to the studio work. After Mr. Wright's death, Davy designed several impressive buildings and produced a fine collection of landscape pastels.

The next incident in Davy's troubled life turned out unexpectedly rough. He developed a congenital disease of the spine, a pinching of the spinal cord that impaired the use of his legs. At Mayo Clinic, after several life-threatening operations, the doctors said he would never walk again. Davy began to feel very sorry for himself and complained about his condition until he met an earthly angel. His near neighbor in the hospital was a former baseball player destined to spend the rest of his life in an iron lung. The man had an undaunted spirit and gave Davy the inspiration he needed to accept his condition with a positive attitude.

From that time on, Davy made people laugh with his many jokes and never complained about his constant pain. He determined to walk again. Soon he could manage with sticks, using a wheelchair when necessary. He returned to Taliesin and, in spite of his difficulties, traveled with some of us to Europe, South Africa, and Japan.

At Taliesin West he built an elegant small apartment and a therapeutic pool. I helped him furnish his apartment and plant the garden surrounding the pool. After Davy's death, his apartment and pool were incorporated into my residence. Because Davy loved flowers, every year I plant the garden with petunias, geraniums, and lobelias in his honor. The bougainvillea and pyracantha have become high trees and the oleanders are profuse with blossoms.

My bedroom has always been adjacent to the pool. One day before Davy's death, Indira and I saw him struggling to get out of the pool. He was trying to grasp the railing but his arms failed him; the spinal cord was being further constricted. Indira had often helped Davy, and he enjoyed her company. I said, "Indira, rush out and help Davy." She managed to grasp him under his arms and to pull him out of the pool.

That day he realized his arms had failed, and he decided to go back to Mayo Clinic. Johnny planned to accompany Davy the next morning and stayed with him that night. During the early hours of the morning I suddenly awoke with a powerful vision of Mr. and Mrs. Wright "bearing Davy on high." Davy was released from all pain as his great spirit soared beyond our earthly Taliesin family.

John deKoven Hill

(Affectionally called Johnny, one of Taliesin's remarkable men.)

From the time Johnny joined the Fellowship in 1938 until his death on June 25, 1996, he made an inestimable contribution to our group, to Mr. Wright's work, and to the world of beauty in design. In going through his papers I found this partially handwritten autobiography. I present it here to explain his origins and the impact of Taliesin when he arrived to become an apprentice.

Background

Born: 5/19/20 Cleveland, O.

Parents: John deKoven Hill (Chicago business office of the Curtis Publishing Co.) and Helen Elizabeth Muckley Hill

Moved to Evanston 1923

Schooling: Grew up & attended high school in Evanston, Ill.

Honor student in high school. Planned to attend Univ. of Virginia when

John deKoven Hill

two sources brought up Taliesin. Only previous knowledge of Frank Lloyd Wright was passing the Baker house (Wilmette) on the way to the beach. It was very appealing, but I never saw the interior. Although I knew Frank Lloyd Wright was its architect I had no idea of what had become of him (1937).

One source of information was Mr. Runge, my geometry teacher at Evanston High. He was my favorite of many good teachers. He made geometry fascinating and crystal clear. He also remembered that a former student, Jack Howe, had

gone to study with Frank Lloyd Wright a few years earlier. This was in the fall of 1937 when I was making plans for college. (Architecture was without question my main interest; music, perhaps, second.) An architect uncle (John Gillett of Mills, Rhines, Bellman, Nordhoff, Lee & Gillett, Toledo, O.) had given me T-square, triangles, drawing board, etc. before I was kindergarten age and taught me how to use them. Many fine castles, plans of our house with layouts of furniture arrangements for parties, and other important things were accomplished, and I developed an ability to easily read plans and understand how they might develop in volume. I think this same ability made me a fast sightreader at the piano.

That fall my father came home with the information that Herbert Johnson (a friend through business) was building a new building designed by Frank Lloyd Wright and further that he had some sort of arrangement for taking apprentices.

This information upset all my plans. I did not find anything appealing or reasonable in modern architecture as I knew it (the Chicago Fair 1932–33). I was attracted by classic architecture and Georgian residences, furnishings.

Stainless steel & white Formica were what came to my mind as the materials for modern buildings—cold, unromantic, lacking any beauty or charm. I finally arrived at the sad understanding that these imitations of the past were not proper for my lifetime and that I had better give up beauty, charm, and romance in favor of cold, (white Formica, stainless steel) modern architecture.

When I finally saw Taliesin, its impact was an emotional revelation and a tremendous shot in the arm. Here was everything I loved all real, never seen before beautiful spaces and forms, mossy stones and fountains, and just enough decay here and there to add to the apparent eternal, no-time period naturalness. And here also was real "nature" everywhere and the civilized organization of farm life right alongside and among beautiful music, elegant dinners, European films, glamorous guests, and, most remarkable of all, Mr. and Mrs. Wright, who as a couple seemed unbelievably made for each other—handsome, stylish, quick to respond—magnetic.

I had cancelled the application to the U. of V. (Not too hard because all I knew was that it had a reputation resting on parties, alcohol, fast living, none of which I knew anything about.)

I managed to reach Gene Masselink at Taliesin. He promised to send all information and enrollment forms, then promptly forgot, I learned later, because he was leaving for Arizona that afternoon—the last one to go. While I was waiting for Gene's response (Dec. 1937) my father went to Tucson for a few weeks' rest at a ranch. He drove up to Phoenix (Jokake Inn) to meet Mr. Wright. He had lunch with both of them. Paid my tuition and enrolled me in the Taliesin Fellowship. He called me that evening to say that he didn't know how much this would contribute to my architectural career, but "a year or two with those two people would be wonderful for anyone." Somehow, during this lunch Mr. Wright arrived at the conclusion that my father owned the Curtis Publishing Co. He introduced me with that bit of information often, probably because it seemed a credit to him as well as to me, whether it was true or not.

He could not see why it was necessary to wait until high school graduation in June until he understood that I was the editor of the school paper. "Social Purposes. Well, that's different."

So I saw Taliesin for the first time in May that year (1938) when Dad, Mother, and I drove to Spring Green to see it. Svetlana (Wright) Peters was our hostess for lunch because Mr. and Mrs. Wright were en route to Russia. (This was the day of revelation for me architecturally and every way.)

On June 17, 1938, without waiting for the graduation ceremony or the diploma, I went to Taliesin to stay. I didn't meet Mr. and Mrs. Wright for another two weeks when they returned from Russia. No theatrical entrance I have ever seen matched their entrance into the Taliesin studio after arrival on the midnight train. Stylish, handsome, electric—they moved rather quickly through the room greeting people as they went. All their exuberance and youthfulness was something I was totally unprepared for.

I was the "baby" in a group of 22 apprentices. It quickly became home. And because I was so young I gained an alternate introduction: "This is Johnny. His father left him on my doorstep in a basket."

When Johnny first came he lived in the room next to mine. Since my wardrobe wasn't long enough to accommodate evening dresses—dresses with trains—Johnny offered to keep them in his tall closet. Five or six of his young high school friends came to visit. Since I was a few years older than Johnny, they were very impressed that he had the evening dresses of an "older woman" in his closet. Many years later one of those boys wrote the musical *Auntie Mame,* perhaps prompted by some early memory of the evening gowns.

Since Johnny and I were to decorate the theater that same weekend, we had his friends pile into the back of the pick-up truck to go exploring for oak and pine branches. We tramped through the autumn woods, found our branches and returned with an excited crowd of boys holding down the collection of branches in the bed of the truck. With the fun of a new experience, everyone helped decorate the theater for the formal evening. After such a weekend, a very impressed group of boys returned to Evanston with stories of the trip to the woods, the formal evening, Johnny's wardrobe, and the baby goats that climbed over the roofs.

Johnny at seventeen came to Taliesin as a tall, handsome blond—"Adonis," Mrs. Wright said. But Johnny was more than an Adonis. He had a very brilliant mind, tremendous talent, and competency in many fields. As Charles Montooth has written:

Joining Frank Lloyd Wright's Taliesin Fellowship as an apprentice architect after finishing high school, John Hill became one of Mr. Wright's most trusted and valued associates. He supervised the mounting of exhibitions in this country and abroad, oversaw the construction of some 69 Wright homes including designing the interiors and furnishing of 20 of them.

Johnny led an amazingly varied life during his long association with Taliesin and Mr. Wright. He managed the vegetable gardens. He ran the dairy farm during the coldest winter on record. He looked after the two Taliesin houses. He directed the Taliesin chorus. He performed classic works on the piano for Taliesin formal evenings and arranged and decorated the spaces in which these events took place.

For ten years he furthered the cause of organic architecture as editorial director of House Beautiful *magazine. He also designed elegant homes as well as an extensive and popular exhibition of model rooms to show people how they might live beautifully. He was responsible for fabric and interior furnishing designs that have been produced and sold throughout the world. He super-vised the selection and production of lines of Frank Lloyd Wright furniture and furnishing designs. All this was done quietly in keeping with Johnny's modest but distinguished manner. Although he had to his credit important buildings and beautiful spaces, one of his last and most beautiful achievements was the simple, graceful, gradual, winding path that leads up the hill to Taliesin from the fields below.*

John deKoven Hill was a true extension of the work and ideas of Frank Lloyd Wright. We will miss his matchless, creative touch.

Johnny, Wes Peters, and Gene Masselink, each for a different reason, were all right-hand men to Mr. Wright. Mrs. Wright called them "The Three Musketeers." They all showed great artistic sensibilities and creativeness, often working together on important projects. Mr. Wright used to say, "Johnny, someday you will play Brahms to my Beethoven." Johnny had a highly cultivated ear for music. Because of his ability to rapidly sight-read he accompanied our musicians on the piano. For many years he also directed the chorus.

When Elizabeth Gordon, editor of *House Beautiful* magazine, sought to recruit an architectural editor, she asked

Mr. Wright for a talented man to help. Mr. Wright sent Johnny to New York, and together Elizabeth Gordon and Johnny transformed the magazine into something beautiful and instructive. He became editorial director of the magazine and published articles and photo layouts of Mr. Wright's work and the work of other architects creating organic designs. Elizabeth and Johnny traveled abroad and brought back many innovations for the magazine, many fresh ideas, such as the portrayal of Japanese *shibui* in all its delicate nuances. The work Johnny did there had an enormous influence both here and abroad as he opened new vistas for beauty in architecture and interior design.

Johnny stayed with *House Beautiful* for ten years. After he turned in his resignation he received this letter from R. E. Deems, Vice President of Hearst Corporation:

Nonetheless Johnny returned to Taliesin after Gene Masselink's death to become Secretary of The Frank Lloyd Wright Foundation. In the late 1960s and early 1970s he collaborated with Wes Peters on houses and palaces in Iran. He also designed several notable houses and created furniture, fabric and carpet designs, and murals.

Upon Johnny's return from New York we worked and traveled together designing interiors for hotels, office

September 21, 1962

Dear John:

It was a sad day for me and for this organization when I received your letter saying that you would be terminating your services with us October 1, 1963.

Dick Hoefer tells me that you are planning to return to Taliesin, feeling that there will be fulfillment in running the Wright school and educating young people. I can readily understand your viewpoint. It is admirable.

However, John, I wonder if you realize how much of an influence you have been these last several years on the culture of this country. You have a rare combination of qualities, and you and Elizabeth have had a vehicle with which to educate literally millions, for the influence of House Beautiful *goes so far beyond its one million circulation. You and Elizabeth have made a splendid team and I would certainly hope that between now and next October you, Elizabeth, Dick, and I would find a way to make it possible for you to not only remain with us but to continue the most important contribution which you have been making to America's taste.*

Perhaps in the next few weeks we ought to get together over the luncheon table and talk more about it.

Meantime, this is a propitious moment to express my appreciation to you for your intense effort over the last nine years. I am taking the liberty of sending copies of this to Elizabeth and Dick.

R. E. Deems

buildings, palaces, houses, and other buildings. Our companionship lasted for over thirty adventurous years. At the time of his death in 1996, Johnny served as Honorary Chairman of the Board of The Frank Lloyd Wright Foundation. Many letters came from friends and former apprentices who spoke of the wonderful things this great gentleman had taught them. Johnny had an elegant manner and dedicated his life to creating beauty in every aspect of daily living. Because of his quiet ways, his sensitivity to people's feelings, and his highly cultivated taste, one friend wrote, "Johnny was one of Nature's Noblemen."

During the last years of his life Johnny reestablished the living room at Taliesin West with the original furnishings Mr. Wright had designed for that space and helped redecorate and revitalize the Cabaret Theater and the Pavilion. In Wisconsin he opened the vistas of the House by eliminating destructive additions made after Mr. Wright's death.

Johnny had such a love of Taliesin that he returned early every spring to see its buildings before the leaves emerged—then to watch the progression of spring as small shoots of ferns and bloodroot emerged from winter mulch, as the fragrance of lilacs, apple, and plum blossoms filled the air and as the leaves of the great oak unfurled over the Tea Circle. Consequently, his many friends established a memorial landscape fund for Taliesin in Johnny's memory.

On a personal level, Johnny had a sense of elegance in all that he did. He had always been looked up to by his peers as arbiter of manners, dress, and good taste. He became our acknowledged authority to approve appropriate new additions to our estates and also to see that repairs to buildings proceed according to Mr. Wright's intentions, as far as he could ascertain that.

The only one who had sway over Johnny in all matters of behavior and good taste was his faithful dog Buppo, a handsome, lovable, creme-colored standard poodle with apricot ears. Once a week Buppo's beauty specialists groom him with a becoming poodle cut. Ever since he was a pup, he and Johnny had an agreement that whatever Buppo did was not only O.K. but also very entertaining.

For the last ten years of his life, Johnny and Buppo were inseparable. This story of Johnny's life would not be complete without the tales of Buppo. As a pup he shredded several of Johnny's straw hats and would appear around the corner of the room with a brim around his neck. Johnny just said, "He's so cute doing it!" Later Buppo ripped up two pairs of Birkenstock sandals. I asked, "Doesn't that bother you?" "Well," said Johnny, "he's so very entertaining when he's chewing them up." Then Buppo ate

Joe Fabris with Buppo and Nicky

117

a Seven-Up can—all but the ends. The veterinarian X-rayed him every day for a week until all aluminum squiggles were eliminated.

When Johnny's life ebbed away, Buppo became my dog, but Joe Fabris, guardian uncle to all the dogs, takes care of Buppo. Joe, a dog lover, understands their language. Now Buppo is companion to Joe but also shares his affections with all of us. None of us will forget the magic current of love that flowed between Johnny and this elegant poodle.

A former apprentice, Liz Conn, wrote a letter at the time of Johnny's death that captures something of the spirit of Johnny and Buppo:

If I were to write a poem about Johnny, there would be green hills continuing into an indefinite distance. A man would be walking towards them on a mist-covered path, the sky gray. A dog with a leaping spirit would be running alongside the man, a shocking white, clear against the gray. But at some point, the man would move ahead and disappear into light just as the gray and the mists clear, revealing a sun-filled opening where the man last stood.

Kenn Lockhart

Recently, when one of our senior members, Kenn Lockhart, died, Charles Montooth wrote such a heartwarming and appreciative account of Kenn's life that I would like to include it here.

Kenn Lockhart: A Colleague's Appreciation by Charles Montooth

Kenn Lockhart was the all around model apprentice at Taliesin. When I landed in Wisconsin at the end of World War II, T-square, triangle, and tools in hand, Kenn was the kindly young man who took me in hand and showed me how to do whatever needed doing. And he knew how to do everything there was to do: draft, build, cook, farm, maintain machinery, pilot a bulldozer or motorbike, stoke the boilers, cut wood, and

Kenn and Susan Lockhart

shovel snow. A tall, handsome, friendly man, he taught us newcomers what we had to know, and he did so with remarkable patience. It is not stretching it to say, as John Hill said, Kenn kept the Fellowship intact, together, functioning, working, and playing. A man of the out-of-doors, he would organize a band of apprentices for overnight camping and a sumptuous breakfast of pancakes, bacon, eggs, and coffee over a hot predawn fire in the Superstition Mountains of Arizona.

Kenn plunged with gusto into all aspects of Fellowship life. He was a musician who sang in the Taliesin Chorus, wielded a strong bass in the Ensemble, and participated on stage in the dances and as a lead performer. He was a charming, impeccably attired host at traditional Taliesin formal evenings. Kenn was much liked and admired in Taliesin's hometowns of Spring Green and Scottsdale where his many activities brought him into contact with community merchants and leaders.

In my early days in the Fellowship, Kenn, along with Wes and Johnny, was the senior sought out for advice on construction and mechanical matters. And, of course, cooking. When Mr. Wright needed something done, whether it was repairs to a client's house or building a hand-hewn door for the living room, he called on Kenn. A finish carpenter, Kenn could make elegant furniture, build fine cabinet work, or turn out scale models of Frank Lloyd Wright's masterful building projects.

Kenn was also the man to have around in a crisis. Swift of action, whether it was to help an apprentice badly injured in the shop or on the job or to rescue a dinner from some hapless cook's unintended disaster in the kitchen.

He never pushed himself as a designer—even though his own house at Taliesin West is one of the finest designs there, featuring the best desert masonry stonework to be found anywhere.

To help us—his architect colleagues and our apprentices—Kenn ventured into the arcane and much-shunned world of specifications. Essential to our practice, he goaded and guided us into the ever-changing building scene of new materials, methods, and practices. He became our conscience of good office practice. Words and their precise meanings were important to him. At Taliesin he kept alive the term "apprentice" at a time when use of the word "student" was in vogue. He insisted on our using the correct names for products and their proper applications. He applied his craftsman's skill to specification writing, winning awards and national recognition for his work and for his efforts as an officer of the Construction Specification Institute.

Bill Logue

Bill Logue is an agreeable Irishman whose temper and sense of humor bespeak the certainty of his heritage. Bill and his wife Sarah had a sturdy Rhodesian Ridgeback named Bamboo. When talking about dogs one day Bill said, "I think dogs can understand what you're saying. Once I had a good pair of freshly cleaned and pressed pants. I went into the kitchen to put them on, but red dog hair from Bamboo covered the floor where he laid. So I stood up on a chair, balancing on the edge of it. Just as I got one leg into the pants, the chair fell, breaking the back of the chair, and also my tail bone. I got up and bellowed, 'I'll kill that dog!' Bamboo bolted right through the screen of the door and disappeared! It took Sarah three days of combing the neighborhood to find Bamboo, a forlorn and starved dog."

I asked Bill if he'd seen a doctor about his broken tail bone. "Sure," he said, "but the doctor just went to the window, stood there with his back to me and laughed, like you just did!"

As a young man, Bill attended Illinois Wesleyan College in Bloomington. A city street ran directly from Wesleyan to Normal College in the connecting town of Normal. It was a perfect setting for rival pranksters. During one football season, Bill, in good Irish form, parked his car in Normal with the intention of painting the sidewalk green. As he emerged from his car with a can of green paint he encountered a policeman who asked, "Young man, what do you plan to do with that paint?" Without missing a beat, Bill improvised, "Sir, I plan to paint my car."

"Fine," the officer said, "I'll stay here and see how it's done." While the highly amused policeman watched, Bill had to paint his car green.

Since coming to Taliesin, Bill's life has been more productive. He plants a large vegetable and flower garden in the spring. As it matures, it furnishes our kitchen with a great variety of fresh vegetables and herbs, and the flowers adorn our dining tables and provide abundant bouquets for all who enjoy picking them. When the frosts of fall spread their white crystals over the garden, the dried corn stalks rustle in the wind, and the last tomatoes hang in frozen red and green globes on the blackened vines, the raccoons, who have spent the summer breaking down the corn stalks to steal the ears vanish into their lairs, and wild geese honk as they fly in formations over the garden on their journey south. Then Bill's thoughts turn to the homeland of his Celtic ancestors.

Every fall he and Sarah pay homage with a trip to the Emerald Isles. There they've found a comfortable cottage in the country, owned by a middle-aged couple. The husband is a powerful hand-gripper for whom it is best to be prepared. The woman is very proper—straitlaced, in fact. One day she appeared in a red sweatshirt. Written across her breast he read the words "Happy Hooker." Bill was flabbergasted. He wondered if she knew what it meant. Later he learned boats traveling along

Bill and Sarah Logue

the coasts are called "hookers." Bill's landlord owns one named "The Happy Hooker."

Bill lives at Taliesin in Spring Green year round, keeping watch over the buildings and the snowy valley and spending time browsing seed catalogs, watching football on TV, and reading in front of a roaring fire. As the soft green buds appear in the spring, Bill pitches energetically into the planting of the garden.

Eugene Masselink

Eugene Masselink, whom we all called Gene, had an optimistic nature. His one complaint about life was that it had "no background music." He made up for this, however, by the exuberant, creative spirit with which he greeted all situations.

Gene, an artist of unusual ability, met Mr. Wright when he lectured at Ohio State University. Gene had just graduated from the Art Department. He and Mr. Wright had an immediate rapport. So Gene came to Taliesin as Mr. Wright's secretary. He had no experience but did his one-finger typing with enthusiasm.

Gene's father and mother were born and educated in Holland. After they were married, they headed for Pretoria, South Africa. On the way Mrs. Masselink gave birth to Gene in Capetown. She became very ill, and Dr. Masselink had to leave her in the hospital and continue on to Pretoria where he had made a commitment to start a dental practice. After a few weeks Mrs. Masselink gained enough strength to travel with Gene. They took the train into the interior. When rolling through remote territory, Mrs. Masselink discovered the baby's luggage was missing. All accouterments—bottles, diapers, clothes, and food had been left on the platform in Capetown. People on the train rallied to supply supplements for the baby. With their help, she and Gene made it to Pretoria where the family stayed for a few years before moving to Grand Rapids, Michigan.

Ben, Gene's younger brother, arrived much later; so Gene, playing alone, developed a very creative imagination. He played a solitary game in the living room, pretending he lived on a great scorching desert. In each corner of the room he made an oasis of a glass of water and a bowl of dates. Panting desperately with hunger and thirst he would drag himself over the searing desert and settle in exhaustion as he reached each oasis. When Gene went to school and college, he turned his creative sights to art. His paintings, which appeared in many one man shows, had a very fresh distinctive style although Hans Hoffman, the famous watercolorist, had been his teacher.

After Gene arrived at Taliesin his style changed as his impressions and observations became more varied. Following Mr. Wright's suggestions, he began to work more in geometric, abstract forms. He designed murals for Taliesin and for Mr. Wright's clients. He studied the nature of wild tiger lilies in Wisconsin and desert cactus and yucca in Arizona. All his observations resulted in spirited designs.

Before Gene's work became more abstract, he had painted a watercolor of birches on the hill across the valley for me. The sunny scene glowed with life. Later we had a disagreement. Gene snatched the picture and tore it to pieces. Being very upset, I cried, "How could you do that?" He said, "God giveth and God taketh away."

One evening after the 1938 movie *Un Carnet De Bal* had been shown in our theater, Gene with great enthusiasm about the film started to run across the hill to Taliesin. The film had given him a real "high." Later as Mabel Morgan and I drove over the hill in the pickup truck we saw the agonized figure of Gene. He had fallen and broken his hip. At the

Eugene Masselink in John Hill's Bantam

Dodgeville Hospital they put in a pin. For weeks he had to lie in bed with a heavy weight on his foot. This left him with a stiff foot and a hip that became more painful in the coming years. He never complained. In fact, he joked about it after that accident, but he walked with a limp, slinging his stiff foot forward as he went.

Gene had a high baritone voice of beautiful tonal quality. With Johnny accompanying him on the piano, he sang German *lieder* and French and Italian songs. As his spirits rose during a song his increased tempo made accompanying him a nightmare for Johnny. Nonetheless, their exceptional talent carried the day.

As secretary and confidant to Mr. Wright, Gene became indispensable. When Mr. Wright legally established The Frank Lloyd Wright Foundation, he appointed Gene secretary.

Gene worked tirelessly at everything he undertook. He lived completely for Mr. and Mrs. Wright and the work of the Fellowship. When getting up early in the morning to cook breakfast, Gene brimmed over with enthusiasm. Wes Peters bought special goodies like blueberries and strawberries to augment Gene's breakfasts. This made the other cooks jealous.

Gene had a very formal side that put him in good stead with the many people who came to the office. When necessary, he served as a buffer for Mr. Wright. One time his formality came in for a lot of kidding. He tried to deter someone whom he knew Mr. Wright didn't want to see. Standing tall with his arms folded over his chest, Gene met the person and said very formally, "I'm sorry, you will not be able to see Mr. Wright today. Mr. Wright is very busy. He's swatting flies!" Mr. Wright could be heard in the next room wielding his fly swatter. When the rest of us would be suffering from hoards of mosquitoes, they never bothered Mr. Wright. Flies were another matter. He got real satisfaction out of swatting them. I also think it helped him relax. Gene had a lot of diplomatic talent, but we never let him forget the swatting incident.

With his great sense of humor he could tell very juicy jokes, but he also could respond angrily when pressed into an unwanted situation. One of the girls who became infatuated with Gene pursued him mercilessly. At an encounter in the dining room their tempers flared. She grabbed a hanging ribbon of fly paper and wrapped it around his head, flies and all.

As Gene delved deeper into the work of the Fellowship, he started a printing press where he not only produced exceptional graphics but also printed *The Square Paper*, which Mr. Wright was writing at that time. *The Square Paper*, a quarterly, documented much of Mr. Wright's philosophy and his critiques of current topics. Gene designed the publication in the shape of a square, and he created all of the graphics.

After Mr. Wright died in 1959, the Fellowship continued to complete his unfinished buildings, including the Greek Orthodox Church in Milwaukee. Gene started to paint the icons—done in beautiful luminous colors. After a hard day's work helping Mrs. Wright with the tremendously complicated transition necessary to carry forward Mr. Wright's work and the business of the Fellowship, Gene painted icons late into the night. He sustained himself with handfuls of candy as he worked. Having become absorbed in Greek Orthodox liturgy, he had decided to study with the priest in order to become a confirmed member of the church. Gene had painted most of the icons and placed them in the gold filigree screen in front of the altar when he died of a massive heart attack in 1962.

Coming so soon after Mr. Wright's death, Gene's sudden passing was a blow to all of us. When we assembled his artistic productions for the archives, it became apparent that he left us an amazing heritage of great works of art. Gene was truly one of Taliesin's remarkable men.

Charles Montooth

Wouldn't you be charmed by a red-haired, freckle-faced fellow like Charles who, upon receiving his first bank account and checkbook at age twelve, sat down and signed all the checks so he'd be ready? After many years of apprenticeship in the Fellowship and more years of architectural practice, Charles is still "ready." The spontaneous charm of his youth has spilled over into creative solutions for beautiful buildings, for the columns he writes for our weekly paper, *The Whirling Arrow*, and for the pleasure he gets and the attention he gives to cooking breakfast for the Fellowship.

On any sunny, rainy, snowy, or foggy morning, the herons and geese at our pond must be surprised as Charles passes by on his four o'clock walk around the Taliesin grounds. A long-time Jeffersonian democrat, Charles is a member of the Frank Lloyd Wright Foundation Board and gives great thought and creative energy to our life at Taliesin.

After his early morning walk, he settles at his computer in the drafting room to spend the day concentrating on designing the buildings while at the same time teaching our young apprentices. Whether working on an athletic fieldhouse or a hotel, an arboretum or an addition for a school, Charles is completely absorbed in his work and dedicated to his creations.

When the rest of us depart for warmer climes, Charles stays behind to brave solitary winters of snow, ice, and blizzards in Wisconsin.

Not so his sociable wife, Minerva, equally absorbed in the work and pleasures of our group life. She accompanies the Fellowship to Arizona and continues her work with apprentices, helping them create programs for our formal evenings, making guest lists, growing flowers for apprentice wedding receptions, or working at whatever needs to be done to enhance the social side of our Taliesin family.

Both Minerva and Charles are dedicated workers—Charles during the day and Minerva at her computer through the still of the night.

William Wesley Peters

When the International Style architects adopted the slogan, "Less is More," Mr. Wright paraphrased it as "Wes is More."

William Wesley Peters, affectionately known to us as Wes, first visited Taliesin in the summer of 1932. When he met Mr. Wright, he already had decided to leave Massachusetts Institute of Technology where he had enrolled in engineering to become a marine architect. Ships fascinated Wes, and he built intricate models

Charles and Minerva Montooth

of famous sailing ships. After his meeting with Mr. Wright, however, he began his lifetime association as a member of the Taliesin Fellowship.

We knew Wes as a handsome, vital powerhouse of a fellow—"a hale man well met," with a lusty interest in all aspects of life. His strength belied the fact he had weighed but three pounds at birth. His mother carried him around in a shoe box! When he arrived to stay at Taliesin, the Fellowship had just started. He and the other early apprentices worked hard to build and furnish new rooms for those yet to come. Mr. Wright saw Wes carrying a heavy oak door and asked, "Boy, where are you going with that door?" "I'm going to make a bed frame for my room," Wes answered. And from his very first day there Wes took the initiative in all the work at Taliesin. With boyish energy, he liked to tackle whatever needed doing. He became a natural leader of the apprentices, and Mr. and Mrs. Wright put him in charge of all kinds of work—in the drafting room, on building construction, or farm work.

Wes fell in love with Svetlana, Mrs. Wright's daughter, whom Mr. Wright had adopted. Svet, as we called her, had matured into a lovely, talented fifteen-year-old. Since Mr. and Mrs. Wright considered her too young for a serious

relationship, they tried to break it up. Wes and Svet eloped, but they realized they should not get married. Wes returned to his home in Evansville, Indiana, where his father was editor of the *Evansville Press*. Svet, using her pen name, Sargon Wilde, went to live with the Crees, a musical family in Winnetka, Illinois. There she and their daughter, Margaret Jean, studied music together. Margaret Jean became a fine cellist who later played with the Chicago Symphony for many years, and Svet became an accomplished pianist and violinist.

The courtship of Wes and Svet continued, with ardent love letters flowing between Winnetka and Evansville. Eventually they married. Mr. and Mrs. Wright, realizing they had made a mistake, urged Svet and Wes to return to Taliesin. From that time on, Wes took a lead in every kind of work. So did Svet. She not only participated in daily chores but had charge of the music program, helping to train and accompany young musicians. At one time she kept Toggenburg goats. She not only milked them daily but also made cheese of the extra milk. In cold weather she kept the newborn kids in her room, but when summer came nanny goats, billy goats, and kids scampered over our roofs.

William Wesley Peters, 1937

Wes and Svet had a son named Brandoch, followed by another boy, Daniel. In 1946, Svet, again pregnant,

Cornelia with one of Svetlana's goats

started driving her boys to Spring Green in a jeep. At the bridge, she lost control of the car and plunged into the swamp. Svet perished, taking her children with her, but five-year-old Brandoch, thrown free and in a state of shock, ran a mile down the road to get help at Richardson's gas station. Sadness swept over Taliesin. Everyone in the Fellowship suffered the loss of this fine woman and her children.

As architectural work flowed into Taliesin, Wes creatively worked out the engineering for Mr. Wright's innovative buildings, many of which had problems other engineers could not solve. Wes did the engineering for the Johnson Wax building in Racine, Wisconsin; the Kaufmann house named Fallingwater at Bear Run, Pennsylvania; Beth Sholom Synagogue in Philadelphia; the Guggenheim Museum in New York City; and many other buildings. Recently an engineer came to the Frank Lloyd Wright Archives to review the calculations Wes had done for Fallingwater. As he studied Wes' notes he was astonished and said they were far ahead of their time. The formulas that Wes had created years ago have only recently become standards of general engineering practice.

Wes, an insatiable reader, had a phenomenal memory for detail. On any subject mentioned he could supply more in-depth facts than we sometimes wanted to know. Nonetheless, we all went to him for information and advice.

Wes was a fine romantic artist and thoroughly enjoyed our pre-Easter sessions when we all sat around painting goose eggs for favors for our guests at Easter breakfast. At one such session Svetlana Alliluyeva, Stalin's daughter who had just escaped from Russia, joined our egg painting party. Svetlana's charm fascinated Wes. He had long held the name Svetlana deep in his heart. After a two-week courtship they married. They had a daughter, Olga, but the marriage soon came to an end. Svetlana left Taliesin with Olga. A magazine article summed it up: "Jeffersonian Democrat Divorces Communist Princess."

Wes, generous beyond belief, used any holiday as an excuse to give multiple presents to everyone in sight. Once Wes pressed me about what I wanted for Christmas. I jokingly said, "A Teddy bear." A package four feet high and three feet square arrived. My Christmas gift! Ten bears—bears with real fur, large bears, small bears, white bears, black bears, and Teddy bears—all wearing extravagant rhinestone necklaces or earrings. Over the years, Wes gave me so much jewelry that I can festoon my entire Christmas tree with lavish rhinestone necklaces, bracelets, and earrings. Always ready for any occasion, Wes kept drawers full of jewelry—some costume jewelry, but also fine watches, Indian bolos, turquoise rings, squash blossom necklaces, concho belts, and special items made of precious jewels that he designed for his close friends.

Wes enjoyed skit parties, limericks, and practical jokes. His close friend, Aaron Green, a former apprentice and long-time associate in San Francisco, once beat Wes with a practical joke. Aaron persuaded someone to call Wes and pretend to be a famous Madam wanting a house designed for her "girls." Wes, genuinely excited about the project, fell for it. He strode up and down the room rubbing his hands together and practically smacking his lips about the fun of such a commission. The great letdown came when after several weeks Aaron had to admit to the joke. For the first time Wes couldn't think of a practical joke super enough to top Aaron's.

For children's parties, Wes could commandeer a gang of fearsome pirates to walk the plank into the swimming pool or dress like Merlin to put on a superlative magic show using the outfit he kept in a secret trunk. He accomplished everything with boyish humor and infectious good cheer. In the drafting room he liked to sing "Men of Harlan" or "The Streets of Laredo." He could recite poetry for hours.

Wes was fearless when protecting Taliesin. During World War II, two FBI men came snooping around the grounds. Wes met them with a shotgun and made them drop their guns and put their hands up. When they couldn't produce a search warrant, he ordered them to leave.

In fact, Wes championed the cause of anyone in trouble. Driving through San Francisco once he drove beside a car where a boy was yelling for help. A gang had the fellow in the back seat, beating up on him. "Stop!" Wes yelled, but they kept on beating the boy. Wes followed them side-by-side on a hair-raising chase until they met a policeman who cornered and arrested the gang in a blind alley. It was a tough gang, and the policeman thanked Wes profusely for his courage.

After Mr. Wright's death, Wes became our senior architect, creating many notable buildings. When Mrs. Wright died in 1985, the stewardship of the Fellowship was reorganized. Wes became Chairman of the Board of Trustees, a position he held until he had a

Wes Peters, 1990

sudden stroke in 1991. For over a week he lay in the hospital asleep like some noble warrior struck down. We of the Fellowship took turns staying by his side until he died peacefully on July 17, 1991.

The Fellowship held a memorial service for Wes in St. John's Catholic Church designed by him and built in Spring Green. A speaker phone broadcast the service to the Pavilion at Taliesin West as it proceeded in the church. People came from all over the world to both places to participate in the celebration of Wes' life, his accomplishments, his sense of humor, and his loyalty to friends.

His former wife, Svetlana Alliluyeva, wrote the following obituary:

"Wes (as he was known) was a man of integrity, honesty, generosity, and kindness. He was a workaholic and was loved by his colleagues. Absolutely unambitious, unselfish, unpretentious, rather shy and silent, never has built a house for himself. Beautiful moments of our brief marriage will remain in my memory forever. He had a good sense of humor and was a romantic; loved Wisconsin and American West, knew its art well and collections. Our daughter is 20 years old, presently resides in Britain. Wes was very much loved by everybody as a man who never pushed others aside for his own gains, rather he would abandon his own gains for the sake of the Fellowship, of colleagues, of friends. As a person, he was charming, kind, quiet, undemanding, and absolutely unselfish. A very rare man, almost extinct qualities. It's so sad he is gone."

Bruce Brooks Pfeiffer

When Bruce came to Taliesin at the age of seventeen, his swift repartee was not always taken seriously. But Bruce, who still speaks in words that dance lightly on the air with the speed of sunbeams and the froth of waves, is a very productive, creative man. Mrs. Wright first discovered his talents and understood his potential.

Bruce is a musician. He plays the piano with a light, sensitive touch. At the keyboard he can portray people's characters with humorous inventiveness, or he can be very serious. He collaborated with Mrs. Wright in working out the harmony for her music. She created the music for many dance dramas, and Bruce helped transcribe it for orchestra.

During one period he masterfully directed our chorus with such inspiring music as *Carmina Burana* by Carl Orff, previously unpublished twelfth-century songs from Henry Adams' collection, and early works of Palestrina.

Bruce also is a dog lover. Magnum, his first doberman pinscher, was not the fierce dog his breed sometimes represents; rather, he was mild mannered and given to carrying mail, Bruce's jacket, or

Bruce Brooks Pfeiffer with Geronimo

a toy. One day he raided the children's play space and came back with a large white bear—a bear just about his size. Fortunately, the children didn't want it, for Magnum refused to give it up.

Like most big dogs, Magnum required as much care and attention as a child. When he was hit by a truck, the vet had to replace a tooth with a very expensive silver incisor. It became Magnum's status symbol. In any case, he and Bruce were a devoted pair, and wherever Bruce went Magnum followed carrying his bear. He never interfered with Bruce's intense professional life, however. Magnum has passed on, but Geronimo, a red doberman, now lies beside Bruce's desk as he writes and directs the activities at The Frank Lloyd Wright Archives.

For many years, Bruce was in charge of serving Mrs. Wright in her dining room. He trained the young apprentices to serve with grace and style. It was the turn of a serious and proper young man to serve Mrs. Wright at a luncheon she had for a very attractive, voluptuous blonde. Her large bosom appeared ready to pop out of her tight décolleté dress. Our embarrassed young apprentice went to the kitchen to ask Bruce what he should do if this happened. Without missing a beat, Bruce advised, "Since it's a luncheon, use your hands, but if it were a dinner, warm spoons would be more appropriate."

After Mr. Wright's death, Bruce began to devote his full time to collecting and cataloging Mr. Wright's work and seeing to the preservation of some 22,000 drawings and 300,000 documents. The archive he created has become widely recognized as one of the greatest of its kind.

While accomplishing all this, Bruce also has succeeded in writing thirty-nine books based on the work and thought of Mr. Wright housed in the archive. He also is an arresting speaker and, because of his now-famous scholarly work, is sought after as a lecturer and TV guest.

Bruce's fame "sits lightly on his brow." To all of us, he is an entertaining, loyal, lovable friend.

Madam Po and Ling

I never understood the excruciating pain of bound feet until I saw Madam Po haltingly walking in her baby-sized oxfords. Madam Po was an aristocratic Chinese lady of the old school. With Mr. Wright's help, her son Ling Po brought her out of China when the Cultural Revolution paralyzed the country. They came to Taliesin where both of them began the adventure of becoming citizens. Ling, having worked in the United States in two architectural offices, had already learned some English, but Madam Po spoke only Chinese. When it became time to appear before the judge for citizenship, the judge asked Madam Po, "Do you swear to tell the whole truth, etc.?" Ling Po answered, "My Mother, she swear."

Madam Po had a small room off the apprentice courtyard at Taliesin West. In order to be near her, Ling designed and built a handsome tent in the desert just beyond her window. Bill Calvert went to visit and asked, "Does your mother like your tent?" Ling conferred with his mother, "My mother, she like," he said. Bill then asked, "Would she like to live

Madame Po and Ling Po

there?" A long conversation in Chinese ensued. Finally Ling translated, "My mother, she say, 'Hell no!'"

Madam Po became an integral part of our family. Because of her painfully bound feet she couldn't participate in physical activities but produced intricate embroidery, made stylish "frogs" for dresses, and created hanging tassels for lamps. With small bits of very ordinary fabric, she could create an elaborate evening bag. During the years when we performed dance dramas for the public, Madam Po and Ling sewed very professional-looking boots of canvas, felt, or leather for all the dancers, sometimes as many as thirty or forty pairs.

When the time came in the spring for all our people to move from Arizona to Wisconsin, Ling and Madam Po were assigned to travel with David Dodge, who laid down very strict rules: no smoking and no eating in the car. Wes Peters decided to play a practical joke on David. He froze some limburger cheese and just before they departed, secretly fastened it under David's seat. As the sun rose to its sweltering midday heat a dreadful stench permeated the car.

David accused the Pos of hiding food in the car. He refused to believe their protest, threatening that they would have to get out and walk. He stopped the car to make a search. When he found the melting limburger cheese under his seat, the Pos were vindicated. David must have recognized this as a prank of his good friend Wes, but he never mentioned the incident.

During our Wisconsin summers, Ling was a devoted worker in our vegetable garden and insisted upon carrying his share of any work. He sewed boots, designed a mural, built a house, created wooden and bronze sculptures, taught our apprentices rendering and perspective, rebuilt an automobile, and designed individual watercolor place cards for two hundred and fifty Easter breakfast guests. Madam Po has left us to join her ancestors and Ling left the Fellowship in 1997 to join a Buddhist monastery.

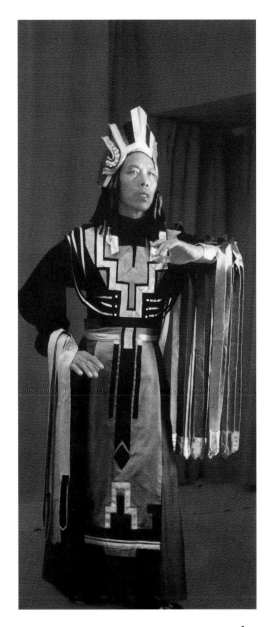

Ling Po in costume for dance drama

Many brilliant architects trained at Taliesin and their stories could fill another book, but some became my colleagues and neighbors when I joined the Fellowship. They have since made their mark as prominent architects.

A handsome couple, John Lautner and his first wife, Mary Bud—a blonde, Nordic Garboesque girl—lived in the room adjoining mine. When she and John, both very tall, entered the living room in evening dress they presented a striking, elegant appearance. Mr. Wright admired their style, but usually said, with a twinkle in his eye, "Sit down, John and Mary Bud, you're throwing the room out of scale."

John, a powerful worker, with rhythmic motions pitched heavy loads of hay to the top of an already laden wagon. For his Taliesin maintenance chore he chose to do steam fitting because it gave him constant access to Mr. Wright. Their many discussions went far beyond the intricacies of steam fitting. When we first started the camp at Taliesin West, John built himself an unusual angled

Jack and Lou Howe, 1993

shelter—a harbinger of the creative work he later did in California. His soaring cantilevered roofs have become famous and his complete originality comes through with every building. John's grown children plan eventually to house the record of his architectural practice at a Taliesin Fellows archive we would like to create at Taliesin West.

John Howe (whom we called Jack) was one of the first apprentices at Taliesin. His mother had attended the Hillside Home School run by Mr. Wright's aunts and had familiarized Jack with all its history. When Jack arrived at Taliesin, he taught himself drafting by spending his evenings studying and tracing Mr. Wright's drawings. He became very adept as a fast and expert draftsman and renderer. For many years he acted as "the pencil in Mr. Wright's hand," coordinating work in the studio. In 1964, Jack and his wife Lou left Taliesin to start their own practice. Lou, a remarkable helper for Jack, is a very efficient and reliable person who had helped Gene Masselink with the secretarial work for Mr. Wright. Together she and Jack established an office in Minnesota. Since that time Jack has produced designs for five hundred buildings during the course of twenty-five years, a monumental task for one man. After retirement he left his drawings and papers to the Northwest Architectural Archives at the University of Minnesota. The memorabilia pertaining to Mr. Wright and the Fellowship have gone to the State Historical Society of Wisconsin.

Edgar Tafel and Bob Mosher shared a room at Taliesin. We considered Edgar, who has a great sense of humor and irresistible charm, as our "Peck's Bad Boy." He pulled off many practical jokes with Bob as his accomplice. One time they made a victim of Jack Howe who lived in a very small room at the top of a two-foot-wide stairway. The room, just big enough for a bed and a drafting table, had very little space. Edgar and Bob managed to get Blackie, Iovanna's wild black pony, up the stairs and into Jack's room. The pony had no room to turn around. When Jack arrived, he somehow managed to back Blackie out of the room and maneuver him down the stairs. Edgar and Bob both became noted architects, Edgar in New York and Bob building for the fashionable set in Marbella, Spain.

Bill Bernoudy and Burt Goodrich lived in the Hill Garden tower. Bill, a charming, cultivated, sociable person who didn't want anyone to know that he took his turn as one of our best cooks, paying great attention to attractively serving every dish. He always looked forward to getting back home to St. Louis for the "Veiled Prophets' Ball." In socially oriented St. Louis, Bill was a very sought-after bachelor. When he left Taliesin he married and became a prominent St. Louis architect. Burt was a quiet, responsible worker. When he left the Fellowship he traveled to the Northwest where he had a thriving practice doing innovative and creative architectural fabric designs.

The Dombar brothers, Abe and Benny, worked tirelessly at any task at hand. Abe was a charter member of the Fellowship from 1932 to 1935. Benny arrived in 1934 and stayed until 1941. Both have had private practices in Cincinnati for years.

Blaine Drake, who married my sister Hulda, had an impressive practice in Phoenix, Arizona. After his death in 1992, Arizona State University acquired his papers and drawings for their archives.

THOSE WHO CAME LATER

Many of the people who worked with Mr. and Mrs. Wright remain at Taliesin as senior staff members of the Fellowship, which is the governing group of The Frank Lloyd Wright Foundation. Since the deaths of Mr. and Mrs. Wright the Foundation has grown into a multifaceted corporation that includes Taliesin Architects, the Frank Lloyd Wright School of Architecture, the Frank Lloyd Wright Archives, Visitor Center and Bookstore, and various departments.

Many of those who stayed to continue the Fellowship, I've already written about—Davy, Johnny, Kenn, Dick, Bill Logue, and Charles Montooth. The group also includes the following people who are highly trained and multitalented. This group of senior staff, trained in every aspect of the work, act as the knowledgeable nucleus for the continuance of the Fellowship ideals and mission.

A new group of dedicated young people are ready in the wings and are carrying on the Fellowship traditions.

Indira Berndtson
Anna Berndtson Coor

Both my daughters spent their early childhood at Taliesin. After a year at the University of Chicago, Indira became a member of the Fellowship in 1962. She worked as secretary to Iovanna Lloyd Wright, then as executive secretary to William Wesley Peters until 1982. Since 1982, she has worked with Bruce Brooks Pfeiffer in the Frank Lloyd Wright Archives. Her duties include assisting in cataloging the collection, working with researchers, and conducting audio and video oral history interviews. She has been Secretary of SOHA—the Southwest Oral History Association—since 1995.

Anna returned to the Fellowship in 1973 and worked as an executive secretary for both William Wesley Peters and Richard Carney. She met and married her husband, Roger Coor, at Taliesin, and they lived here until 1986, when they moved to Phoenix to begin Roger's own architectural practice. Anna returned to teaching.

During their years at Taliesin, Indira, Anna, and Roger participated fully in community life: singing in the chorus, helping with maintenance, cooking, and performing in the Taliesin Festivals of Music and Dance.

Tom and Effi Casey

Tom Casey, a principal architect in Taliesin Architects, serves as dean of the Frank Lloyd Wright School of Architecture. His leadership has earned the School formal recognition as accredited programs at both the bachelor's and master's levels, which continue to draw apprentices from all over the world.

Tom was an apprentice to Frank Lloyd Wright from 1950–1959. His special interest and knowledge in structural engineering contributed to the realization of major Frank Lloyd Wright buildings. For the better part of the 1970s Tom worked as the architect-in-residence in Tehran, Iran, supervising several buildings designed by Taliesin Architects, among them the Pearl Palace for H.I.H. Princess Shams Pahlavi.

His wife, Effi Casey, is an artist and musician who came from Germany to join the Taliesin Fellowship in 1966. In addition to overseeing the advising program for apprentices she is the director of assessment for the School. Effi, also the director of music at Taliesin, currently serves on the board of trustees of the Frank Lloyd Wright Foundation.

Heloise Crista

Heloise, born in Japan and educated in Canada and California, studied applied arts at UCLA when she discovered and read Frank Lloyd Wright's *An Autobiography*. Drawn by the warmth, beauty, and spirit of his work, she came to Taliesin in 1949 to study his philosophy and architecture and to become part of the Taliesin Fellowship.

Unexpectedly, she spent the following years largely in dance and costume design for the Taliesin Festival of Music and Dance. In 1956 she made a bust of Frank Lloyd Wright. It was not until 1978, however, that Heloise made a decision to become a sculptor and followed her own self-made path toward that end.

Heloise Crista with her sculpture

Mainly of cast bronzes, her sculpture also includes those made of welded Corten steel and fabricated sheet metal. One may observe that her sculptures show her dance training in the strong flow and movement of her cast pieces. Her works reflect her thoughts and concerns and her ideas of individual evolution.

Heloise has had several shows, and she exhibits her works at Taliesin West where they are available for sale. Her pieces are seen and admired by visitors from across the United States and abroad.

David and Anneliese Dodge

David Dodge joined Taliesin in September 1951, after two years' study at Oberlin College majoring in music and the arts. He now serves on the Frank Lloyd Wright Foundation Board, is a principal of the Taliesin Architects, and on the board of the Wagner Festival--the first non-German to be so elected. He has been very active with church, theatre, opera house and concert hall design for Taliesin Architects, as well as many residences. David has clients in Arizona, Massachusetts, and Minnesota and is

David and Anneliese Dodge with Mrs. Wright

currently preparing construction drawings for a grand lakeside country house in Minnesota. David also lectures and conducts tours for important visitor groups.

In the 1960s and '70s Mrs. Wright asked him to help with the scoring of the Music for the Taliesin Festival of Music and Dance.

David and Anneliese met in Montagnola, Switzerland when the entire Fellowship spent a second summer there. Anneliese has become the manager of the highly successful bookstore at Taliesin West. After starting with a portable stand, Anneliese has developed the most active bookstore specializing in Frank Lloyd Wright and organic architecture. Anneliese and David are just completing Poppyfield II, their own home at Taliesin West.

Joseph Romeo Fabris

Joe Fabris, a Canadian chemist who graduated from the University in Manitoba, worked in an industrial lab in Canada. He came to the United States to join the Fellowship in 1948 in order to study architecture. He is a master builder, accomplished designer, and the architect of a number of buildings. He works tirelessly at improving the buildings of our two Taliesins. In so doing he supervises and teaches our young apprentices with patience, consideration, and understanding.

Joe is interested in poetry, canoeing, and skiing. He is a dog lover, "uncle" to all dogs, who speaks their language and trains them to be agreeable community members.

Marion Kanouse

For many years, Marian Kanouse, an officer of the Farmer's State Bank of Spring Green, Wisconsin, took care of the Fellowship accounts. She personally advised many apprentices concerning their financial matters, helping them with necessary loans, and providing financial counsel. After retiring from the bank in 1984, Marian joined the Fellowship as assistant treasurer and continues to unsnarl Taliesin finances.

Marian, a dog lover, can't deny cookies, jerky, or other treats to all Taliesin dogs. As they hover under her desk, they are always assured of a snack or several snacks.

Marion Kanouse

Susan Lockhart

Susan Jacobs Lockhart, as the daughter of Wright clients for the Herbert Jacobs' houses—I (the first Usonian) and II—was a friend of the Fellowship from an early age and joined as a member in 1958 after graduating in art education from the University of Wisconsin-Madison and working in New York. Her passion for the creative arts was expressed first in music as a pianist and dance with the Taliesin Festival of Music and Dance for ten years, then as the Taliesin Architects' graphic designer. In the last ten years she has concentrated on creating her own abstract geometric designs in leaded and deep-carved glass, stained wood, and fabric applique for clients and galleries. Her tableware and small glass sculptures are licensed products marketed nationwide.

Susan's activities in the Fellowship range from cooking, music, and teaching and advising in the School, to membership on the boards of The Foundation and Taliesin Architects. She regularly organizes cultural events and productions open to the public at both Taliesin and Taliesin West.

Sarah Logue

Sarah and Bill Logue had long shared an interest in Mr. Wright's architecture and Mrs. Wright's philosophy. After ten years as frequent guests of the Fellowship, in 1957 Mr. Wright invited them to join the Fellowship with primary responsibility for the farm at Taliesin. With Sarah's background in art and social work and Bill's in economics, their activities in the Fellowship, in addition to farming, became many and varied.

Sarah spends the summers in Wisconsin supervising apprentices on the weekly worklists and graphics, as well as acting as year-round supervisor of the household budget, ordering, and shopping. Her time spent in the 1970s and early 1980s as companion to Mr. and Mrs. Wright's daughter, Iovanna Lloyd Wright, took her for extended stays in New York, California, Connecticut, and Paris.

Minerva Montooth

Minerva Montooth has been associated with the Taliesin Fellowship since 1947. Mr. Wright invited Charles and Minerva to have their wedding at Taliesin West in 1952 and was host for the evening. Minerva acted as Mrs. Wright's personal assistant from 1962 to 1985, which included working with her on her many writings. She traveled extensively with Mrs. Wright, including trips within the United States, Europe, and South Africa. Currently Minerva coordinates the many diverse activities of the Taliesin Fellowship and School; serves on the admission, social and education committees; and helps advise apprentices and review their portfolios. For many years she has kept a photographic record of Taliesin life and each summer is the weekly correspondent from Wisconsin for *The Whirling Arrow*.

Frances and Stephen Nemtin

Frances, raised in India, graduated from Bryn Mawr College and came to Taliesin in 1946 directly from the directorship of the Milwaukee Art Institute and just after mounting a beautiful Frank Lloyd Wright exhibit. She and Stephen met in 1959 when he came to Taliesin from Montreal and were married six months later. Together they worked in Iran for three years in the early 1970s on

Stephen and Frances Nemtin

Tony Puttnam (standing in the back) and crew rebuilding the Sun Cottage at Taliesin West, c. early 1960s
Crew left to right: Gary Herberger, David Dodge, Tom Olson (with his back to the camera), Kamal Amin bending over the concrete form

three large Taliesin projects. One included landscaping a 77-acre site above the Caspian Sea for Princess Shams. Since their return they have supervised care of the grounds of the two Taliesin estates. Frances also has designed all the Wisconsin summer garden flower beds, restored two prairie areas, and planned the replanting of many trees in Wisconsin lost to severe storms. They ardently work with others as stewards of the Wisconsin estate to maintain its beauty and usefulness. Frances' other enthusiasms are pottery, music, and writing.

Stephen, a principal in Taliesin Architects, has recently focused on health care issues as they related to Alzheimer's disease, designing two Alzheimer residences and a hospice. These buildings all express organic principles in innovative solutions for the human condition. Stephen's newest design is a residence of bold form and airy spaciousness poised on a ravine above Puget Sound.

Anthony Puttnam

Tony joined the Fellowship in 1953 and is now an architect and landscape architect who heads Taliesin Architects' Madison, Wisconsin office. He masterminded the building of Monona Terrace, a civic project that Mr. Wright first designed in 1939, which finally came to fruition under Tony's direction. Tony is an accomplished photographer, whose photo of Taliesin West appears in this book.

John Rattenbury

John joined Frank Lloyd Wright in 1950, and over a period of almost ten years, worked on fifty of Mr. Wright's projects, including the Guggenheim Museum and the Marin County Civic Center. Serving as a principal in the firm of Taliesin Architects, he has designed several hundred projects in the United States and overseas. His work ranges from hotels and civic centers to residences and large-scale master plans. He also teaches design, lectures around the country, and is currently writing a book on the work of Taliesin Architects.

Dr. Joseph Rorke

"Dr. Joe," attracted by the philosophy of Mrs. Wright, joined the Fellowship in 1956 in order to work with her. He became the Fellowship physician and took good care of us for many years. He retired from medical practice in 1985 and now edits and publishes our weekly in-house newsletter, *The Whirling Arrow.* In early morning he takes the mail to town, does daily grocery

Kay and John Rattenbury on their wedding day

shopping, and returns to give expert tours to visitors. He has created several computer-generated videos on the architectural ideas of Mr. Wright for use in educating our visitors and others.

Dr. Joseph Rorke and daughter Shawn Rorke Davis

Arnold and Dori Roy

Arnold, a principal of Taliesin Architects, is a master builder and accomplished photographer and craftsman. For many years he built fine cabinetwork for Taliesin. Arnold is a member of both the Taliesin Preservation Commission Board and The Frank Lloyd Wright Foundation Board. As vice president of the board, he chairs the facilities committee. He represents us locally in Scottsdale on many community commissions and still manages to carry a heavy load of architectural work. Currently he is the architect for the Gold Mountain development and golf course project—1,200 acres on the east slope of the High Sierras in California—and other buildings throughout the West.

Dori, a devotee of Mrs. Wright's philosophy, has always been a consummate team player, doing everything from managing the Taliesin Architects' office to assisting Mrs. Wright, dancing in the performances, and participating in the chorus and recorder groups. Currently, she manages the telephone communications.

Tom and Effi Casey

Arnold and Dori Roy

How Sir William, a handsome white-haired man in his sixties, worked his way into Taliesin remains unclear to me, but the stories of his brief stay have become legendary. He dressed elegantly in silk shirts and other expensive clothes and could be very charming, as he dropped names of the internationally renowned from all walks of life.

When he asked to join the Fellowship, Mrs. Wright hesitatingly agreed, but she later had doubts about her decision when he admitted to having been jailed for "tax evasion." From the beginning, the title "Sir" was questionable, but we went along with it. In his photo album he appeared in the pictures of many famous family groups, including the John F. Kennedy's.

Sir William had a house in a small New Mexico town and claimed to have a ranch (which no one could ever locate) on the Pecos River. At first he worked very hard teaching the apprentices how to recondition and use our old printing press. Then, when we moved from Arizona to Wisconsin in the spring, Sir William spent much time on the road traveling back and forth to Arizona, always by night. That fall at Taliesin West he presented Mrs. Wright with a Rolls Royce. After giving her a ride up to the mountains, he said, "I'll take it to Scottsdale to be serviced." Several times Mrs. Wright asked when her car would be ready. "Soon," he'd say. She never saw it again.

A Jesuit priest brought a mini-circus to Taliesin West for a performance in the pavilion, our theater for music, drama, and dance. The entire circus, including the priest, a wire-haired terrier, and a black bear named Dorothy, lived in a very small van with an unbearable stench. Being in heat, Dorothy became dangerously obstreperous. When the priest said he planned to give Dorothy away, Sir William offered to take her to his "ranch."

That evening he put Dorothy in the back seat of his Mercedes with a sheet of 3/4" plywood as a barricade between her and the driver's seat. Although everyone, including the priest, advised against this arrangement, Sir William drove off. A few miles down the road he stopped for gas. Dorothy, with one sweep of her paw, shattered the plywood. The priest, called to the rescue, coaxed Dorothy back to Taliesin and confined her in a backstage room. Horrified, Mrs. Wright said, "Get that bear off this property immediately."

The Phoenix Zoo offered to keep Dorothy until Sir William could find a truck to transport her to his "ranch." The next week he left Taliesin with Dorothy chained in the back of a pickup truck. When he returned (by night, of course), he said, "I left Dorothy in the back room of my friend's jewelry store in Albuquerque. My friend's 12-year-old son takes her for a walk every day through the streets of the town!"

Having concluded this operation, Sir William bought $3,000 worth of jewelry in Scottsdale, paying for it by check. He sported the jewelry around Taliesin for a week then took out another $3,000 worth of jewelry on consignment. When the store insisted on payment, Sir William said, "I don't owe you a cent. Here's my canceled check for $3,000 to prove it."

At that point he went off to New Mexico but not before he'd talked one of our apprentices into giving him $7,000 for which he said he'd get the young man a great deal on a car. He never produced the car. When the Scottsdale jeweler sent a man to New Mexico to collect his $3,000, Sir William graciously received him in his home. After an amiable visit, Sir William said, "Why don't you go and have a bit of lunch. When you come back I'll have your money." When the man returned, Sir William, with the sheriff at his side, had the poor fellow arrested for "intent of extortion."

Once during his stay at Taliesin, Sir William drove a car to New York for Mrs. Wright's granddaughter, Eve, who was studying there. He immediately set about charming Eve's elderly landlady. Even though Eve warned her about Sir William's escapades, the landlady, captivated and flattered, would not listen. The last we heard, Sir William had moved in with the landlady after Eve left. He cultivated a relationship with a circle of her elderly lady friends and in good time, with promises of sure-fire investments, relieved them all of their money.

We have not seen or heard from Sir William since, but we certainly haven't forgotten him.

LATER YEARS

TRAVELS ABROAD

Europe

Even though the Fellowship travels across the country twice a year between Arizona and Wisconsin we never lose the zest for further adventure.

After Mr. Wright's death, we made several European tours. For the first trip in the summer of 1964 we divided into two groups of 25 each. The first group flew to London and took the channel train to France. In Paris five Citroen station wagons were rented for the summer at a cost of $500 each. With five people in each car we had a rolicking trip through France, Belgium, and the Bavarian Alps. Then we continued down steep mountain roads along the Adriatic Coast to Yugoslavia, where we stayed on the romantic island of Sveti Stefan.

This island village has no roads, only winding walks and steps that climb among the picturesque stone cottages as they ascend the hill to an open flowery terrace and a small chapel at the top. Once pirates held this island stronghold. During World War II, legend claims,

Mrs. Wright, Cornelia, and Charles Schiffner
at a market in Rome

Picturesque Sveti Stefan

posts on the causeway to the mainland were lined with heads of enemies. Despite its violent history this charming island gives no hint of anything but tranquillity. Making Sveti Stefan our base, we explored the mountains of Montenegro and especially the town of Cetinje where Mrs. Wright was born. The road to Cetinje leads up a steep mountain where wild fig trees grow among the boulders and an occasional small stone house settles into the rocks of a precipitous slope.

Arriving at Cetinje was an emotional experience for Mrs. Wright. We visited the town square where, as a child, she read to her blind father, the chief justice of the country. She pointed out the miniature palace where she remembered sitting on the laps of the young princes as they told heroic stories. We tried to find the house where Mrs. Wright had lived, but since she was sent to be with her sister in Russia when she was nine, her only memory was of climbing an apple tree in the back yard. We visited several houses but found no apple tree.

Touring across a high plain we came to a special mountain, and trampled the low grasses and fragrant herbs as we climbed the path to the top where we arrived at the statue of Marco Milanoff, Mrs. Wright's grandfather who is still

John Amarantides conducting the chorus on the terrace at the American School in Montegnola
Left to right: Leslie Lockhart, Shawn Rorke, Frances Lockhart Nemtin, Cornelia, Heloise Crista

highly honored throughout the country for having driven the Turks out of Montenegro.

When our idyllic stay at Sveti Stefan came to an end we drove up the Adriatic coast to Split where we embarked to Italy. Driving through Italy we enjoyed the hill towns, the sunny countryside, the Ufizzi Gallery in Florence, the Sistine Chapel, and other historical sites of Rome.

Mrs. William Benton and Mrs. Wright at "Fiera Falls"

Upon returning to Paris we met the second group as they arrived from London to take over the Citroens for their tour of the Continent. Our group flew back to Taliesin. For $2,500, fifty of us had transportation for summer tours of Europe!

For the next two summers we rented the American School buildings in Montegnola, Switzerland. In order to continue the architectural work, drawings were put on microfilm for transportation. We set up a drafting room in one of the school laboratories where work could proceed at a serious pace. Chorus and ensemble rehearsals and our formal Saturday evenings continued. But to everyone's pleasure, all maintenance chores were eliminated in favor of complete service by the school's staff.

We picnicked in flowery mountain meadows, sometimes by a waterfall which Mrs. Wright christened "Fiera Falls," in honor of her newly acquired Great Dane. On weekends we explored the flea markets in Italy, the fireworks on Lake Lugano, the Wagnerian festival at Beyreuth, the coffee and pizza houses, the ski resort at St. Moritz, and all the pleasurable adventures of a summer holiday in Europe.

Africa

Mrs. Wright was asked to lecture in Durban, South Africa. Eight of us joined her. We boarded the *Michaelangelo* for a carefree ocean voyage to Naples. Taking a plane in Milan we flew to Addis Ababa, Ethiopia, over lush countryside sparsely dotted within encompassing circular adobe walled settlements of round adobe-thatched huts. When taken to the site of the hotel where we thought we had reservations, we found ourselves on the outskirts of town, looking at a pile of rubble for a yet-to-be-built hotel! So much for reservations!

Instead we enjoyed the ambiance of a new Sheraton. In this ancient town we visited Haile Selassie's poor sleepy caged lions and explored the vast but impoverished market where sleazy Japanese scarves floated from the ceiling. All about the market men sat cross-legged sewing colorful designs on white gauzelike fabric with amazing speed and dexterity.

The air in this high altitude is exhilarating. The Ethiopian people, who have small-boned, regular features are very handsome and gracious. Fine looking young men employed by the hotel pleaded with us unsuccessfully to sponsor

Mrs. Wright at a market in Nairobi

them in America, as their country is very poor.

When leaving, we waited on the airfield for departure to Nairobi. I was seated on the plane next to a very heavy black man. When I expressed surprise to see the American Army planes on the field, he became furious. He said they shouldn't be there and pointed out that he was a Communist from Guinea, where Russian planes stood on the field. Throughout the trip he managed to

149

elbow and kick me, so I was glad to disembark in Nairobi.

Nairobi turned out to be our favorite stop. We piled into the tourist trucks for safaris to see giraffe families, lazy lions sleeping in the sun, cheetahs with cubs, zebras, fast-traveling, graceful gazelles, and always herds of wildebeests.

Nairobi is a great place to shop for native crafts. We enjoyed seeing how stunning and stylish the clothes looked displayed on the African mannequins. The casual way of life revealed itself at the lunch hour when hundreds of men flung themselves on the lawn of the town square for siesta.

We flew on to Durban, passing on our way the phenomenal sight of Mt. Kilamanjaro as it suddenly arises from a flat plain. Our pilot circled its glaciers, with the wings of the plane tipping toward icy cliffs. We arrived in Durban during race week. The hotel terrace was crowded with elderly English people sipping tea as they rocked in turn-of-the-century wicker furniture. The ladies all wore big hats and old-fashioned finery. Seeing the privileged gathered for race week increased an overwhelming prevalent sense of class and apartheid. As a relief we shopped the market for Zulu crafts and beadwork and marveled at the endless tables loaded with pungently

fragrant heaps of ground spices being sold by East Indian shopkeepers.

In the evening Mrs. Wright gave an hour long lecture at the university. When she pressed the issue of equality of all democratic people the excited students gave her a standing ovation. We were invited to an outdoor Shakespearean play performed by blacks in their own inimitable way. This superb show with a special flavor of native interpretation was later presented in Europe and America.

The next day, upset by the oppressive atmosphere of apartheid, Mrs. Wright, to the consternation of the university hosts, insisted we return to Nairobi where we spent another pleasant week before going to Europe and home.

Japan

In 1967 some of us again accompanied Mrs. Wright to Japan where she hoped to stop the destruction of the threatened Imperial Hotel, which Mr. Wright had designed in 1915. Generally Mrs. Wright received "red-carpet" treatment but the hotel management were inimical to saving Mr. Wright's famous building and didn't show Mrs. Wright the respect she deserved. Groups of architects, trade unions, contractors, and many other

Japanese tried to help her save it by offering donations of all labor and materials to completely rebuild the hotel to its original splendor. The adamant management could not be deterred in destroying this historical, sculptural masterpiece in favor of an ordinary concrete and glass high-rise.

However, we visited the Kabuki Theatre for a spectacularly artistic performance, after which our friends took us backstage to meet their most distinguished actor.

Our guide, who realized we were avid shoppers, took us to a Japanese market not frequented by tourists. Colorful small shops lining the street sold elegant kimonos, jewelry, hair pieces, obis, men's and women's robes etc.—a shopper's paradise! In Kyoto we visited renowned palaces and gardens. But the rarest treat turned out to be a Geisha performance shown only once a year since 1872 with magnificent costumes, music, and acting.

We had lunch on the second floor of a peasant-style restaurant. One side of it was completely open with a view of a slow-moving, tree-lined river below. Waitresses in colorful kimonos kneeled on the floor in front of us to prepare food on pieces of heavy iron from peasant hoes. These irons can be detached from

A scene from "Kamo-gawa-odori," which is a Geisha dance performance in Kyoto that has been performed only once a year since 1872

the hoe handle for use as cooking utensils when the peasants work in the fields.

Upon leaving, we descended the steps to the main floor, a tiled lobby. The kitchen, enclosed at one end of the room, was flanked by a square booth with about a 2 1/2 foot wooden base enclosed above with glass. Along the same wall a shoulder-high tiled trough ran to the end of the room. Out of curiosity I went to investigate this glass-enclosed booth. To my astonishment it contained a toilet! The trough beside it was plumbed for hand washing.

This scene hit me very personally. For years I had had a nightmare of sitting nude in such a glass enclosed booth. The surrounding room was crowded with people. Suddenly the sides collapsed, leaving me completely exposed. The sight of this similar Japanese booth struck me so deeply that I burst out in an uncontrollable combination of laughter and tears. To explain this to others was completely impossible. Since this surge of deep emotion, I have never again had that nightmare.

Back in Tokyo, the hotel was crowded with young brides and

grooms who came to be married, hopeful of capturing good luck before the building's destruction. Some brides wore beautiful traditional kimonos but the height of fashion seemed to favor American evening gowns.

Many Japanese students who are a part of our extended Taliesin family came to Tokyo to honor Mrs. Wright. They all tried to help save the Hotel. Mrs. Wright invited them to a Taliesin-style cocktail party. She sent Heloise Crista and me to the department store for liquor, Wisconsin cheese, Ritz crackers, and other American goodies. The lower floor of the store was a Mecca for both Japanese and foreign foods. After several hours and a great struggle with language, we returned triumphantly with everything on our list. At the cock-tail party our former girl apprentices and the wives of the men wore elegantly embroidered kimonos. They enjoyed their American cocktail party and all paid homage to Mrs. Wright. Our Japanese students, all of whom are very loyal, continue to send new students to share the experience of our two Taliesins.

Building a Palace

Shortly after Mr. Wright's death, Wes received a commission to design a palace for the Princess Shams, the elder sister of the then-Shah of Iran. Wes enlisted the help of Johnny. Before Johnny had gone to New York, Mr. Wright had relied on him to decorate many of his buildings. Johnny, who had exceptional talent as a decorator and designer, created many beautiful interiors for Mr. Wright's buildings.

Wes and Johnny produced a remarkably original and romantic design for the Palace. They detailed all the custom furnishings—including beds, chairs, tables, and lighting fixtures. After renting the American School for the season, the Fellowship spent the summer in Montagnola, Switzerland. Johnny and I gathered fabric samples both from the United States and from Europe. We hung them on the walls of a small room where Mrs. Wright could select color schemes for the Palace. Having lived in Russia on one of the czar's tea estates in the Caucasus, she intuitively understood the kind of colors that the princess might enjoy. Her selections made a great hit.

Wes called his creation for the Princess the "Pearl Palace," a very appropriate name considering the pearl-like lights and skylights that enhanced the roofs, the large translucent dome that covered the main rooms, the interior gardens and fountains, and a smaller dome that embraced the swimming pool.

The Princess Shams was a devotee of the American scene, so we had all the furniture built and upholstered in the United States. Even the interior plants came from a nursery in California where a dedicated lady, Hela Norman, had carefully groomed them for a year before accompanying them on an aircraft to Iran.

How Wes came to be in Iran

The whole story of the palace reads like an Arabian Night's tale, beginning with the heritage of Sheik Nezam Amery, who had apprenticed at Taliesin in the 1950s, and who had recommended Wes as an architect to the princess. Nezam's mother, Baloul Mafi Amery, came from a distinguished and aristocratic family in Iran. At 14 she married Prince Nosrat Saltaneh, brother of the last Qajarieh

Sheik Nezam Amery

153

King, but it did not turn out to be a happy marriage and four years later she divorced him.

Chaperoned by her uncle she traveled by caravan to southern Iran to claim her inheritance of her father's villages. There she met and married the much older Sheik Kazal Khan, who ruled the south of Iran, the region of Kuzistan and all the southern tribes.

The Princess Shams' father, Reza Shah (then Shah of Northern Iran) invited Nezam's parents to visit Tehran, but once there they found themselves under "house arrest." They were given luxurious quarters in Tehran and Shemiran, and Nezam was born when the Sheik was seventy years old. Nevertheless, after ten years the Sheik died under mysterious circumstances. To avoid an uprising of the Southern tribes, his body had to remain temporarily in Nezam's mother's family cemetery until Princess Sham's brother, Mohammad Reza Shah, became King after his father was sent into exile by the Allies during the Second World War. Then proper official funeral ceremonies were held for Kazal Khan in Najaf, Iraq.

Nezam became the architect and friend of Princess Shams. When the Princess decided to build a palace, Nezam suggested Wes as architect, knowing that his romantic genius would create a masterpiece.

The Princess and her pets

Princess Shams was a very beautiful, sensitive, and cultivated person with impeccable taste. In the palace, Wes took into account her appreciation of animals and birds. He designed gold bird cages in the form of octahedrons, tetrahedrons, and other polyhedron forms for the exotic rare birds of the aviary. For the princess' many miniature dogs Wes made an elegantly designed railing not more than a foot high to surround any small dog hazard. Before the completion of the palace, the princess lived in a villa that Nezam had designed. Her animals surrounded her. A cocky miniature parrot liked to get down from its perch and strut around the room. One day we heard that a cat had eaten the little parrot. Our Italian friend, Romano Raffo asked, "Whose cat was it?" "The Princess' cat." "Oh well," he said, "then it is a family affair."

In the evenings the princess invited us to dinner at the Villa. The princess had both a Persian and a French kitchen from which her staff served delicious meals. After dinner everyone watched a movie, usually an American Western, the princess' favorite. Her Royal Highness watched from her chaise lounge, her little dogs cuddled in the folds of her elegant handpainted chiffon dress. Others sat around the room deftly cracking and eating pumpkin seeds. As the evening progressed, people slipped from their chairs to sit comfortably on the floor in ancient Persian fashion. Often the movie lasted until midnight after which the princess conducted business, reviewing the work in progress on the palace and laying plans for her other businesses. She expected all dinner guests to attend these sessions, which lasted until the early hours of the morning.

Tom Casey supervised the palace construction. After late business sessions, he had to drag himself out of bed early to start work on the palace. He and his wife Effi had a young naive houseboy named Mogadan. Even though practically a child, Mogadan and his wife had just had a second unwanted baby. Effi advised him to go to the clinic that the Shah had established in Karaj. When he returned, Effi asked what advice his wife had received. With delight he told her that his wife had been given a bottle of birth control pills, and she was so pleased that she took them all that same night!

Ancient craftsmanship, modern tools

The building of the palace blended two cultures. Modern design and modern equipment were used simultaneously with the skilled work of men plying ancient crafts, such as hand molding a geometric plaster border without the use of instruments. Before Romano Raffo from the Carrara Marble Company in Italy installed the marble floors, the workmen sat on the earthen floor for lunch. They spread out large 18-inch rounds of flat bread on which they broke chunks of another type of bread. With small braziers they brewed tea to complete their meal.

Romano Raffo made his men carve seven white marble bathtubs for the princess before they finally had a pure white tub without a blemish. Johnny and I helped in the development and implementation of all furnishings, always with the princess' careful consideration of each item selected and of the constraints of the budget. For the palace many of the draperies, bedspreads, and upholstery were hand-woven.

The linen orders included tablecloths for outdoor parties thirty meters in length and wide enough to reach the grass. It was customary for guests to serve themselves one course at a time, then slip the plate under the table in order to partake of the next course.

Many in the Taliesin Fellowship helped design murals and do working drawings. Workers from many countries helped build the Palace. Women from Vienna came to put together the crystals for the magnificent chandeliers that Wes and Johnny designed; men from the Uffizi Gallery in Florence worked on goldleafing the walls; marble workers came from Italy; sound equipment men from England; John Ferlin arrived from San Francisco to install kitchen equipment; and workers from Pakistan, India, Japan, Germany, and many other countries joined the work force.

The travails of landscaping

It fell to my lot to work out the landscaping. The head gardener had studied in Germany and had worked all winter laying out a plan. The princess asked me for a list of shrubs. Without my knowledge, she purchased hundreds of shrubs very early in spring and insisted I get there to supervise the planting. The frozen ground was still covered with snow and slush. When I arrived, workmen had not completed the roads and paths.

My arrival antagonized the head gardener who wanted to implement his own plan. When I tried to lay out some of the paths and flower beds, he grudgingly had his men drive in marking stakes. By the next morning all stakes had disappeared. I decided to save the shrubs by "heeling" them in or placing the plant in a trench and covering with soil and mulch until spring. About fifty gardeners followed behind me, each carrying a pot and waiting for me to place his offering. But with the head gardener's sabotage nothing went well.

To make matters worse, one morning as I talked to him I stepped back into a hole that should not have been there and tore the ligaments around my ankle. At the hospital the medical staff applied a cast without even cleaning the mud off my foot! Back at the hotel, the house doctor came to see me. He insisted the cast should come off and took me to another hospital where I sat in a wheelchair in a corridor while the doctor removed the cast, still without any attempt to wash away the mud. Thereafter he came every morning to massage my foot.

Cornelia in Iran at a fish hatchery just before she injured her foot

In the afternoon he sent his nurse, who insisted on bathing me by lathering me from head to foot. Since she had the ripe odor of one who had never heard of deodorants or shaving, my bath in this steamy room became unsolicited confinement. I suggested she didn't need to come, but she couldn't be discouraged and insisted on bathing me until I left Iran. Then her real interest became apparent. She coveted my evening gowns that hung on the bathroom door for want of closet space elsewhere. My intrepid bather asked if she could try them all on to see how she could make some for herself.

When staying in the Arya-Sheraton Hotel in Tehran, I wrote the following letter to Heloise Crista at Taliesin. An artist accomplished in many fields, Heloise trained as an architect in California before she came to study with Mr. Wright. Over the years she has worked on architectural designs, developed creative programs of dance coordination, made costumes for public performances, and, in the last few years, has devoted her time making extraordinary, inspirational sculptures.

Dear Heloise,

Here I am halfway around the world lying in bed with nothing to do but eat, sleep, and keep my foot up as high as possible. The situation is not conducive to losing weight. Each time I call room service, I explain exactly what I want but it never gets here the same way twice. If I say "no toast," I not only get toast but Iranian bread and croissants, complete with an assortment of delicious preserves of fig, cherries, strawberries, quince, plums, honey, or others. Last night I asked what vegetable they had and they said "spinach." "Fine, I'll have some." So the tray arrived without spinach and the waiter just shrugged and said "no spinach, madam." The doctor advised me to drink a double cognac before meals and to eat yogurt. Well, the cognac is a great idea and although I can't take that much at one time I keep it beside my bed and put a disinfecting spoonful into everything I drink. As for the yogurt, it is delicious in the morning but as the day wears on it becomes more and more "goaty," which leaves no doubt as to its origin.

One day I bought a beautiful blue glass vase with a glass frog for my room with the idea of giving it to Effi when I left because she admired it in the store. People have been keeping me supplied with lovely flowers. Yesterday I asked the maid to throw away the dead ones, and she made off with the vase. This morning I asked the housekeeper for the vase and that created quite a furor of people tramping in and out of the room, looking under the bed, in the closets, on the balcony, etc. Needless to say, the vase just isn't here, but the comedy it's creating is very entertaining.

All the garden layouts that you helped with have really come into their own—now that I'm incapacitated. Since the princess is capricious about what plants and how many she buys, I constantly have to alter the scheme of things, but having the large-scale drawings makes red penciling easier. All the boots you've been giving me have also come in handy, what with the long siege of cold weather and muddy work at the site. Now that I'm in bed, the weather has suddenly turned hot with temperatures ranging between 75 and 87.

Tomorrow, with the help of crutches and by keeping my foot elevated in the car, I'm going to the palace with my doctor. He's terribly nice and wants to see the palace but also is accompanying me just to see that I'm O.K. Iranian doctors all seem to study in Switzerland, Germany, England, or the United States. They have trim figures, are usually quite handsome, look dapper in their clothes, and most of them have a very elegant manner. As a rule the Persians are a handsome people. They are very sensitive to appearances and facial surgery is very popular. Both H.I.H. and Queen Farah have had their faces redone. In her early pictures the queen had a full round face. The later photos show the lower part of her face as quite slender, and she now is very attractive.

Love,

Cornelia

Even fairy tales must end

We started work in Chalus (a resort on the Caspian Sea). The buildings included a tea house and guest houses for another palace. Johnny and I worked on the interiors. Effi and Tom drove me to Chalus to see the rice fields, citrus groves, and houses with their thatched roofs. The tea house is perched on the ancient site where a Persian army once had a sentry post during the Roman invasion. This building, an incredibly beautiful jewel, rises from a rocky pinnacle overlooking the semitropical valley by the Caspian Sea.

Mrs. Wright called me, saying she needed me at Taliesin, so I left Iran. Stephen and Frances Nemtin took over the supervision of the buildings and the laying out of the gardens. Working with a new, more competent head gardener Frances did a wonderful job of completing the landscaping for both the palace and the grounds at Chalus.

Wes also designed a campus of magnificent buildings for Damavand College in Shemiran, Tehran, Iran—a girls' school run by Americans. Building started, but the revolution interrupted. I only hope the present regime appreciates and preserves all of these masterpieces designed by Wes and brought to fruition by the Taliesin Fellowship as a contribution to Iran's ancient culture. All of Wes' buildings have a touch of romance, but none have ever topped the inspired, imaginative creations of the buildings in Iran born of the collaborative efforts of architect Wes, designer Johnny, and others of us from the Taliesin Fellowship.

As two creative geniuses Wes and Johnny made enormous contributions to the work of Mr. Wright, to the growth of the Taliesin Fellowship, and to the thought and architecture of the world. Both had a great sense of beauty and devotion to the organic concept of life. Wes produced creative, romantic buildings based on his advanced engineering know-how. His beautiful auditoriums and churches are masterful acoustical

Damavand College

*Second palace at the Caspian Sea
for Princess Shams*

Tea House under construction

designs. Johnny's sensitivity to design not only produced remarkable interiors for Mr. Wright's buildings but his knowledge, disseminated to the world by his unusual editorial directorship on *House Beautiful* during the 1950s, gave a fresh impetus to design. Ezra Stoller, famous architectural photographer, who worked with Johnny on the magazine has written:

Working as we did, a wonderful relationship developed. In his gentle way John brought out the best in me and his unique contribution to House Beautiful *and through it to the taste of this country and beyond cannot be measured, and continues to this day.*

Wes and Johnny, with mutual respect, collaborated on many projects. Their combined work on the Pearl Palace resulted in a completely original organic design of unsurpassed beauty. They created every aspect of the building including furniture, fabrics, carpets, gold aviary cages, crystal chandeliers, fountains, and cascades. The integration of all these elements represented the culmination of years of dedication and expertise in organic design of these two very remarkable men, brought together at Taliesin through their desire to work with Mr. and Mrs. Wright.

More Tales

In September 1992, we had a reunion celebrating sixty years of Fellowship. Our alumni work as architects throughout the world; they come from every type of lifestyle, every religion, and every class. Over the years Taliesin has included as apprentices a princess of Thailand, a prince of the Vatican, a baron, an Italian marquis, and a sheik, along with many others from humble origins.

We all serve one another in Taliesin life, but the prince had trouble with this. Once when his turn as "family server" came up, Mr. and Mrs. Wright had invited a marquis to dinner. The prince flatly refused to serve. Mr. Wright called him to the room and asked, "What is your problem?" The prince drew himself up and announced, "A prince never serves a marquis!" Needless to say, Mr. Wright quickly dispelled this idea, and eventually our prince learned to work shoulder to shoulder with everyone.

People arriving at our reunion, coming from as far away as India, Japan, Iran, and Europe, reminded me of some of their past experiences in getting to Taliesin. A fellow from Bogota, Colombia, had never experienced anything but a tropical climate until he arrived in New York during a severe winter. Dressed in his thin southern clothes, Joaquin Sicard met blasts of icy winds that pierced like knives stabbing from all directions. In a panic he ducked from one doorway to another. Eventually he arrived in Buffalo to stay with a cousin who owned a bar. Most of Joaquin's knowledge of the United States had come from gangster movies. He arrived at his cousin's bar late in the evening just as the place closed. All the patrons had left except two men who still sat at the bar. They started a fight that, true to the movies, ended outside in a shoot-out that terrified Joaquin. When he finally arrived at Taliesin, he enjoyed an unexpected, peaceful existence in the United States.

Our apprentices from foreign countries usually had interesting accounts of their past. Joaquin, an especially good story teller, related this tale about life in Colombia: When he went into the jungle to shoot monkeys he aimed at one partly concealed by foliage. The monkey fell at his feet and as she lay dying, with a pleading look, she stretched out her arms to hand him her baby. He never forgot the eyes of that mother, he said, and he never shot another animal. After his stay at Taliesin, Joaquin returned to Colombia to start an architectural practice.

Many former apprentices have unusual stories of how they heard of Taliesin or how they received word of their acceptance from Mr. Wright. Mansinh Rana from India said that after writing to Mr. Wright, he kept expecting a reply that never came. A postal strike paralyzed India. When the government became inundated with mail, it announced that anyone expecting correspondence could go to the post office to look through piles of letters. Mansinh's friend, a philatelist, sorted through the

Core of the Fellowship. Wisconsin studio picture taken shortly after Mr. Wright's death in 1959.
Front row (left to right): Gene Masselink, Tom Casey, Louis Wiehle, Cornelia Brierly, Jack Howe, Wes Peters,
Davy Davison, Kenn Lockhart. Back row: Joe Fabris, Charles Montooth, John Ottenhiemer,
James Pfefferkorn, Ling Po, Kamal Amin, John Rattenbury, Bruce Pfeiffer, David Dodge

mail for foreign stamps. A red square on the corner of a letter attracted him. It was addressed to Mansinh Rana from Frank Lloyd Wright—Mansinh's invitation to join the Fellowship! After a rewarding stay at Taliesin, he returned to India where he became the chief architect for New Delhi. Now he is Dean of Architecture of a new Indian university.

Other seemingly providential occurrences brought apprentices to Taliesin. When Fay Jones, as a college student, heard that Mr. Wright would receive a medal and speak at the opening of the Shamrock Hotel in Houston he traveled south to Houston, hoping to hear the lecture. As he entered the hotel lobby he found himself, to his discomfort, in the midst of a group of formally dressed, famous movie stars of the caliber of Clark Gable, Spencer Tracy, Cary Grant, and others. Feeling completely out of place, Fay ducked down a hallway. Just as he thought he'd escaped, a door at the end of the hall opened. Frank Lloyd Wright, with flowing cape, emerged swinging his cane. An obviously frustrated man from the American Institute of Architects who had just presented Mr. Wright with a gold medal stood in the doorway, calling, "Come back, Mr. Wright, we're not through."

"No," said Mr. Wright, "I've had enough."

Fay now found himself in the predicament of being alone in the hallway with Mr. Wright. Trying to be less conspicuous, he flattened himself against the wall. Mr. Wright walked up to him and asked, "Boy, what's your name?"

"Fay Jones."

"Jones, that's a good Welsh name, the name of my ancestors. Come with me. We're going to look at this building." Together they walked about the lobby while Mr. Wright pointed out details with his cane and criticized the building.

Soon he had the entire Hollywood contingent in tow. Mr. Wright thoroughly enjoyed his audience.

Fay, already overwhelmed at his good fortune, could hardly believe it when Mr. Wright asked him to join the Fellowship. He has always remained a loyal follower and has achieved fame for his achievements as a creative architect, designing in his own unique style but always giving credit to his mentor, Mr. Wright. Since that day in Houston when Mr. Wright received the Gold Medal, Fay has come full circle; in 1990 he received the same honor, the Gold Medal of the American Institute of Architects.

Such stories abounded at the 1992 reunion in Spring Green. Renewed friendships strengthened alumni ties to Taliesin—ties that will help keep the ideas, influence, and memory of Frank Lloyd Wright alive and the Fellowship family strong.

CHARISMA AND TALIESIN MAGIC

AN INNER SOURCE

A reporter once asked the question, "What was the nature of Mr. Wright's charisma that attracted so many talented and loyal people to remain for years in the Fellowship?"

The question has no simple answer. Mr. Wright must have been born with a great capacity for perception. His life-long quest led him to understand the inner nature or the essence of things—of natural phenomena, of materials, of animals and plants. And most of all, he was intuitively perceptive of human nature. During his childhood, a family of powerful and superior people lavished much love, attention, and discipline upon him. They instilled in him an integrity that he pursued with courage and determination. Every building became a challenge of bucking tradition, pioneering new areas of building, captivating the imagination of the client, and training workmen to use new materials and building methods.

By overcoming difficulties and facing challenges head on, he developed a quiet, inner power. His creativity applied to everyday matters. He constantly amazed us with his fresh approach to every aspect of life, from contouring a field, to hanging a Japanese print, to running the road grader or setting a Thanksgiving table. He believed in beautifying every daily act. Along the way, he developed great charm.

Many times Mr. Wright arose from the ashes of tragedies with an unbelievable determination for rebirth. Since his enjoyment welled up from some deep spring, his balance wheel was humor. When watching a Disney cartoon, a Western, or seeing W. C. Fields play in *Never Give a Sucker an Even Break*, his rich laughter was infectious.

Having grown up in the late Victorian era, he had all the gracious attributes and manners of an aristocrat of that time. He appeared extremely graceful when swimming in the river, ice skating on the pond, or dancing at a formal party. Most particularly, he enjoyed picnics as he guided us into distant woods and meadows, often directing a spontaneous road building, instructing the apprentices in fine building, or explaining the essence of the structure of a tree.

I believe his magnetic charisma came from the depths and breadth of his inner development. Something of the many facets of his being appealed to different levels of people. It was not unusual to hear an apprentice proudly announce, "I'm just like Mr. Wright." This simply meant that he saw some small facet of his own being as a reflection of one of the many highly developed attributes of his teacher.

Mr. Wright devoted all his time and resources to the Fellowship, never sparing himself where either work, time, or money were concerned. It is not surprising that his loyalty was reciprocated, because his charisma resulted from the synthesis of a profound nature.

*Mr. Wright's last picnic with the Fellowship
at Pinnacle Peak, Arizona, 1959*

The magic

Since 1934 when I stepped off the train in the sleepy Depression town of Spring Green, the years have unfurled with a crescendo of fulfilling adventures shared with Mr. and Mrs. Wright and with a family like no other on earth. This life, sometimes challenging, often exhilarating, has unfolded in an atmosphere of beauty, mystery, and the magic of the two Taliesins.

The magic is there in Wisconsin when lightning illuminates our buildings, when spring lilac buds emerge from black winter branches, when wild cranes and migrating Canadian geese soar from the lake to mingle with passing clouds. It is in sunlit rooms of the house and deep shadows of its extended eaves. It is in songs and folktales of our people as we travel back and forth to Arizona.

Yes, it is at Taliesin West, too! It is there at night when the bronze dragon, resting on a tall desert rock by the breezeway, breathes a great gust of welcoming flame, sends brilliant sparks to infinity and lights the mysterious sloping walls. It is there in the midst of a bright sunny day when we are suddenly drenched by a black cloud that rolls up from the valley to bedevil our roof with rain and hail. It is there after the storm when a strange yellow light makes glowing balls of the prickly cholla cactus beyond our walls. It is there in the laughter of the young people who gather to recount desert adventures. It is in the Taliesin tales that I have recounted and in many stories left untold.

Magic is all around us. Perhaps it is because the buildings, the landscaping, and the life are one; they have grown out of the earth by the stupendous efforts and inspiration of Mr. and Mrs. Wright and the hard work, enjoyment, and dedication of all the young people who have helped build our remarkable structures.

Then too, there is the creative spirit of the Welsh bard, Taliesin, who still hovers over us.

RESOURCE NOTES

 PHOTO CREDITS

Taliesin Fellowship Heads West

The Two Taliesins

Taliesin West

The Children

Tales of My Own

Partners in Adventure

The Partners

Center Color Section

Page A: Mr. and Mrs. Wright, 1956. The Frank Lloyd Wright Archives.

Page A: Olgivanna Lloyd Wright, The Frank Lloyd Wright Archives.

Page B: Taliesin, Wisconsin. Photo courtesy Tony Puttnam.

Page B: Tea Circle, Taliesin, Wisconsin. The Frank Lloyd Wright Archives.

Page B: Taliesin entrance court. The Frank Lloyd Wright Archives.

Page C: Taliesin West, Winter 1939. Victor Cusack photo courtesy The Frank Lloyd Wright Archives.

Page C: Taliesin West, Spring 1998. Arnold Roy photo courtesy The Frank Lloyd Wright Archives.

Page C: Original Taliesin West detail drawing on brown craft paper by Frank Lloyd Wright. The Frank Lloyd Wright Archives.

Page C: Original Taliesin West detail drawing on brown craft paper by Frank Lloyd Wright. The Frank Lloyd Wright Archives.

Page C: Painted rendering of Taliesin West original building site. The Frank Lloyd Wright Archives.

Page D: Taliesin West. Photo courtesy Tony Puttnam.

Page D: Painted panel of original site plan of Taliesin West that still stands in the living room. The Frank Lloyd Wright Archives.

Page E: Dance drama performance. The Frank Lloyd Wright Archives.

Page E: Mary Magdalene, a dance by Iovanna Lloyd Wright. Heloise Crista (standing) Susan Lockhart (kneeling). The Frank Lloyd Wright Archives.

Page E: Hillside Theatre interior view of curtain, Taliesin, Wisconsin. The Frank Lloyd Wright Archives.

Page F: Easter celebration balloons tied together. The Frank Lloyd Wright Archives.

Page F: The baba and pascha cheese. The Frank Lloyd Wright Archives.

Page F: Sending Easter balloons aloft. The Frank Lloyd Wright Archives.

Page F Easter breakfast on the terrace, 1953. The Frank Lloyd Wright Archives.

Page G: The Pearl Palace in Iran. The Frank Lloyd Wright Archives.

Page G: Interior scenes of the Pearl Palace. The Frank Lloyd Wright Archives.

Page H: Cornelia is standing in the center of the second row. The Frank Lloyd Wright Archives.